JESUS
in
His Own
Perspective

JESUS
in
His Own
Perspective

An Examination of His
Sayings, Actions, and
Eschatological Titles

Ragnar
Leivestad

Translated by David E. Aune
Foreword by Martin Hengel

AUGSBURG Publishing House • Minneapolis

JESUS IN HIS OWN PERSPECTIVE
An Examination of His Sayings, Actions, and Eschatological Titles

Library of Congress Cataloging-in-Publication Data

Leivestad, Ragnar.
  JESUS IN HIS OWN PERSPECTIVE.

  Translation of: Hvem ville Jesus være?
  Bibliography: p.
  Includes index.
  1. Jesus Christ—Person and offices.   2. Jesus
Christ—Messiahship.   I. Title.
BT202.L43413   1987   232'.1   87-25474
ISBN 0-8066-2297-0

Manufactured in the U.S.A.   APH 10-3513

1   2   3   4   5   6   7   8   9   0   1   2   3   4   5   6   7   8   9

Contents

Foreword

This is a courageous and necessary book. At a time when New Testament criticism is occupying itself largely with peripheral issues such as literary genre, sociological backgrounds, and far-fetched religio-historical parallels, it dares to advance to the historical and theological center of Christianity: the question concerning Jesus himself. The book is excitingly written, understandable to a broad readership of interested nonspecialists, and eminently readable in the translation by David Aune. The scholarly trappings have been limited to the necessary minimum, improving the book's readability.

The author is at once critical and self-critical. His criticism of the reigning skepticism toward questions about Jesus will certainly give offense. Indeed, for this reason the book is to be welcomed—it reminds us that standing behind the New Testament texts are real people, bearing witness based on trustworthy tradition that Jesus himself was a man of flesh and blood who followed God's call, affected the world as no other, suffered a very human fate, and thereby fulfilled God's mission. Leivestad rightly attacks a number of "sacred cows"; the so-called "Q community," for example, or certain speculations about the Son of man and Jewish messianic "dogmatics" (nonexistent in that form). Above all, he addresses critically German New Testament studies since Wrede: he resolutely examines the questions concerning Jesus' claim and authority, and the behavior that led to his death—questions explained adequately only by the consciousness of his messianic call. He is self-critical as well, refusing a "Jesus-psychology" or speculation concerning Jesus' "inner life." One notes on every page an impressive knowledge of the contemporary Jewish background, as well as modern gospel research. Especially gratifying is his challenge to the reader that we cannot understand the Gospels (particularly the synoptics) without a basic historical confidence that they tell the story and message of Jesus as Messiah of Israel.

I hope, above all, that the book will encourage many young, interested Christians to ask their own ongoing—and, in the best sense of the word, historical-critical—questions about the man Jesus and his messianic efficacy.

MARTIN HENGEL
Tübingen

Translator's Preface

Professor Leivestad is an independent thinker (in the best Norwegian tradition) whose scholarship is known and respected throughout the international fraternity of New Testament scholars. The English translation of this book, originally published in Norwegian in 1982, now makes Professor Leivestad's careful, critical, yet constructive scholarship available to a much wider audience. The author's studies on the Son of man question, previously published in Norwegian, English, and German in various European journals, constitute one of his major contributions to biblical scholarship. He was one of the first to realize, contrary to the accepted opinion of most New Testament scholars, that the Son of man designation could not have been a messianic title in pre-Christian Judaism. This view, which has found steadily increasing acceptance on both sides of the Atlantic (though still resisted by some German scholars), has important implications for the study of Jesus and the Gospels.

Professor Leivestad was willing to read through a draft translation of his book, catching a number of errors and making a number of additions and improvements. The translator is also grateful to

Professor Reidar Bjornard (at one time a fellow student with Professor Leivestad at the University of Oslo), emeritus professor of Old Testament at Northern Baptist Theological Seminary, who spent several hours discussing numerous translation problems. Finally, I wish to thank my wife, Mary Lou, who helped me work through a number of problems in translation and expression.

DAVID E. AUNE

1

The Question

How did Jesus regard himself? What role did he intend to play? In this book I try to treat the classical theme of *Jesus' messianic consciousness* once again. I dare not promise that we shall come any nearer a solution than the many others who have discussed the subject previously. The problem is discouragingly difficult, but it so clamors for the attention of those who study the New Testament critically that it is impossible to avoid being troubled by it. Perhaps I write this book as much to put my own thoughts in order as to inform the readers about a subject of which they know little or nothing. Even while writing, I continue to struggle with a question that is so open that I do not know how my answers will eventually turn out. There is always the risk that as soon as the book is finished I will have an irresistible urge to rewrite it!

Is it really possible to give a critical answer to the question of who Jesus wanted to be? If the task is understood as an attempt to search the heart and soul of Jesus, to analyze his thoughts and feelings, or to penetrate his mental processes, then we should quit before we start. There is certainly a considerable amount of evidence which tells us about the reactions and responses of Jesus in various situations. Some is in the form of direct descriptions of his anger, sorrow, disappointment, joy, devotion, and the like. Other evidence consists of statements by Jesus himself, which more or less clearly disclose his frame of mind and feelings. A good share of this evidence appears to be firsthand, probable, and reliable. This evidence is important for every critical investigation of Jesus' life and work, for if there is no possibility of attaining any psychological understanding and insight, his person will be an unapproachable enigma and his proclamation abstract and distant. It means a great deal for us that the Gospels tell about a person of flesh and blood whom we think we can get to know and become attracted to (perhaps repelled by as well!). But the sources are too fragmentary and uncertain for us to push further into the mind of Jesus. The images conveyed by the sources are too schematic and idealized, and the settings of Jesus' words are too hypothetical for us to formulate reliable notions of Jesus' inner conflict and development.

But our task is not to describe the personality of Jesus. It is actually more concrete. What we shall attempt, based primarily on his own sayings, is to find an answer to the problem of whether he was consciously playing a particular role. Did he regard himself as a prophet like other prophets or the final, decisive prophet of the end time? Did he think of himself as the chosen Messiah (however the term is understood)? Is there any other figure or idea in Jewish expectation of the future which provides a better key for understanding why he said what he said or did what he did? Does Jesus' self-designation "Son of man" provide any clues?

Perhaps Jesus did not want to be identified with any role or expectation at all, either because none of them really was suitable or because he did not attach any vital significance to his own person. It is not unreasonable to assume that a critical analysis of the material with the aid of the methods ordinarily utilized by historical and literary criticism ought to make it possible to answer questions of this kind. Those who are not New Testament scholars (and I intend to write so that the book makes sense to them as well) quickly react by finding the problems fairly superfluous. For them the answer is perfectly obvious: Jesus was the Messiah announced by the prophets. That is the message of each and every writing in the New Testament and that is what he himself said. But even a layperson, when he or she gives a little thought to what the concept "Messiah" really represented, knows that the answer is not quite so simple. Was not the Messiah a new David, a king, who would restore the kingdom of Israel? Was that the kind of Messiah Jesus wanted to be? The problems begin to multiply as soon as one answers, "No, he wanted to be a Messiah of an entirely different type." Finally, it is not at all surprising that a number of modern scholars vigorously dispute the view that Jesus thought of himself as the Messiah. They often speak in terms of a "messianic" self-consciousness of Jesus, but put the term "messianic" in quotation marks, to indicate that they do not understand the term in the same way as those who more or less uncritically think that the confession of believers that Jesus is the Messiah corresponds to what Jesus himself had thought and intended.

From the very first, the church has proclaimed that Jesus was Messiah. That Jesus was raised from the dead was synonymous with the fact that God had installed or confirmed him as Messiah. It is a problem for research why the resurrection was so interpreted, a problem we must mention, but cannot take up for separate consideration. However, we cannot avoid dealing with the problem of whether that confession was based on Jesus' own words and deeds in the period preceding his death.

2

The Sources
and Their Use

For all practical purposes, only the four Gospels provide us with historical information about the life of Jesus, though of course the whole New Testament informs us about what believers thought of him. At the same time, the New Testament is a primary source for early Jewish conceptions, alongside of Jewish literature which spans several centuries. There are many difficulties connected with the use of Jewish sources. As a rule, it is difficult to date them and to decide whether they really illuminate the ideas which prevailed at the time of Jesus. Also, it is often uncertain whether they represent widespread conceptions or the particular eccentric views of a small group or an individual author. The sources give us an extremely variegated picture of early Judaism. It was neither standardized nor unified. There was no Jewish "orthodoxy" in the time of Jesus. Incontestable doctrines were extremely few (e.g., Yahweh is the only God, Israel is the people of God, God's will is revealed in the Law). Even if everyone believed that God wanted someday to bestow mercy on his people and save them, there was room for all kinds of ideas and speculations on how this would be accomplished. Ideas about what would happen in "the latter days" were extremely varied and even contradictory. It is fairly misleading to speak of *the* Jewish eschatology, for a systematic teaching about the last things simply did not exist. In order to decide how relevant the comparative material actually is, the decisive factor is whether traces of comparable ideas are present within the New Testament. For the most part, we can assume that motifs which appear to have been unknown to the New Testament authors were also foreign to the setting to which Jesus belonged. This is a sufficiently sound reason why it is unnecessary to deal here with all the eschatological figures or roles which occur in Jewish visions of the future or end-time speculations. Those referred to in the New Testament are sufficient. A special problem is due to the fact that we sometimes suspect that Jewish authors have censored some of the texts which suited Christian purposes, but which could not be approved by rabbinic Judaism during the early Christian period.

Otherwise, it is hardly necessary to say much about the critical way in which the Jewish sources must be used. However, we must explain how the Gospels will be used as sources for the life and teachings of Jesus. Even a layperson cannot avoid noticing that the Gospel of John gives a completely different impression than the other three Gospels. It cannot be used as a historical source on a par with them. The Gospel of John is a distinctive proclamation about Christ in the form of a gospel. The *form* can delude us into reading it as a historical report instead of as a Christological presentation. Naturally the author has made use of certain historical traditions, but he had no intention of narrating history or reproducing Jesus' own words. If we occasionally hit on historically reliable information, it is more or less accidental and due to old traditions within his sources. By and large we are limited to the three synoptic Gospels. However, we cannot simply assume that they provide us with authentic information. If we compare them, we quickly discover that they disagree in many instances. Moreover, scholarship has clarified the fact that their agreements are essentially due to literary dependence. The generally accepted view is that Matthew and Luke have used the Gospel of Mark as a primary source. "Matthew" is not identical with the apostle Matthew, even though the unknown author has borrowed his name. The title can simply have arisen from the fact that this document names the tax collector who was called to discipleship "Matthew," while Mark and Luke call him "Levi" (Mark 2:14; Luke 5:27; Matt. 9:9). To indicate which gospel was meant, someone could have called it the Gospel of Matthew, that is, the gospel which names the man "Matthew" instead of "Levi."

The evangelists wrote their gospels long after Jesus' death. All their data were derived from community tradition. We have little concrete information about how the material was transmitted during the earliest period. Words of Jesus and episodes from his life were regularly referred to in appropriate situations, such as in connection with worship (cf. 1 Cor. 11:23ff.), in moral instruction, in discussions with opponents, and so on. Even the story about Jesus (i.e., the *gospel* with the popular meaning "good news [about Jesus]") had its place. When preaching to people who knew nothing about him, just who this Jesus was had to be explained. This report took fairly fixed forms long before anyone thought to write them down, and the oral story was still in use long after the first written gospel was available. When Luke or Matthew depart from Mark, it is just as likely due to their preference for an oral tradition with which they are familiar, as to the possibility that they are making conscious editorial modifications ("improvements") in Mark. Since Jesus himself wrote nothing, we have no guarantee that a single traditional saying is an exact reproduction of what he said on a particular occasion. This means that we must always be wary of squeezing too much out of singular formulations and individual sayings. But it does not imply that we must give up and say that we cannot know what Jesus preached. Radical critics currently insist that in each case positive reasons must be adduced for accepting a traditional saying as an authentic word of Jesus. Traditionally, the opposite principle has been followed: traditions are to be accepted as authentic as long as there are no pressing reasons for placing them in doubt. In my view this is both simpler and more correct, for the character of the sources makes it very difficult to adduce unassailable arguments that a particular saying *must* have been uttered by Jesus and by no one else.

One widely used criterion of authenticity is, to be sure, that a saying is genuine if it diverges both from what another Jew could have said and from attitudes prevalent in Christian communities. But this can only be used to determine a minimum of authentic sayings, and this minimum could well consist of eccentric, exaggerated formulations which should not be regarded as typical. For that matter, some Jewish scholars maintain that there are scarcely any sayings of Jesus that could not have been expressed by another Jew. That is an assertion not easily disproved. Conversely, one must hope that the disciples learned so much from listening to Jesus that their own proclamation was influenced by his. It is reasonable to assume that much that was attributed to Jesus could have been said by others as well, both Jews and Christians. It is not the individual sayings that radically set Jesus apart, but the general tenor of his teachings. It is the overall picture of the preaching of Jesus which is original, and that in both a positive and negative sense, i.e., both by what is said and by what is missing. "No man ever spoke like this man!" (John 7:46). This overall picture then becomes the surest criterion for evaluating the individual sayings in the tradition. There are a good number of sayings which awaken skepticism because they do not fit the overall picture of Jesus, but harmonize better with conceptions appropriate to the Christian community or the evangelists.

If I should have to argue constantly for the authenticity of the evidence I work with, the book would become unreasonably bulky and difficult to digest. For the most part, I will simply leave out traditions which I and many other scholars suspect are not authentic. The sayings of Jesus are generally more reliable tradition than the stories about him, and they also have greater significance for our task. But an observant reader will quickly discover that parts of the sayings tradition are not considered in this investigation. That is due most often to the fact they do not help us with our problem, but at times the reason is that it is too uncertain whether such sayings really originate with Jesus. In some cases, doubtful traditions must be considered because they are obviously important for our problem.

Most discussions of this kind emphasize the idea that a tradition is "well attested" because it is found in several relatively independent sources. It is obviously important that the whole picture be supported by many sources, but, when it is a question of the authenticity of individual traditions, it matters little whether the attestation is strong or weak. No tradition is so strongly attested as the story about the miracle of the loaves; nevertheless, for other reasons it ends up among the evidence I find impossible to use. There are, on the other hand, several parables which are attested in just a single source, but which I unhesitatingly consider authentic. That does not mean that all parables must be judged authentic, but most of them clearly bear the imprint of having been created by an incomparable master of the parabolic art. Typical form, characteristic emphasis, and relevance for the historical situation of Jesus are much better guarantees of authenticity than broad attestation.

Unlike most scholars, I do not take into account the hypothetical common source of Matthew and Luke referred to by the designation "Q" (or "Sayings Source"). There are reasons for believing that *some* of the material which these evangelists have in common in addition to Mark existed in written form, but it is impossible to reconstruct a written source. All talk of the "Q community" and its theology is relatively meaningless because, among other reasons, it is unthinkable that there existed a community which had no other traditions about Jesus than those found in "Q" (i.e., the material shared by Matthew and Luke but not derived from Mark). For example, Q lacks the passion story!

It is also appropriate to say a few words about the utilization of particular Jewish sources, because also in this regard I differ to a certain extent from the majority. In my opinion it is methodologically inexcusable to use the central section of 1 Enoch (Ethiopic Enoch), which is called the *Similitudes,* as a source for Jewish conceptions at the time of Jesus, at least if its ideas are not supported by other witnesses. This ought to be mentioned, because the Similitudes (1 Enoch 37–71) are the only Jewish writing which uses "Son of man" as a designation for an eschatological actor. The figure is introduced in 1 Enoch 46 in a clear reference to the well-known vision in Daniel 7:13-14:

> I saw in the night visions,
> and behold, with the clouds of heaven
>   there came one like a son of man,
> and he came to the Ancient of Days
>   and was presented before him.
> And to him was given dominion
>   and glory and kingdom,
> that all peoples, nations, and languages
>   should serve him;
> his dominion is an everlasting dominion,
>   which shall not be destroyed.

In Daniel 7 the figure like a human being is a symbol for Israel, "the saints of the Most High" (v. 27), in contrast to the four terrifying beasts which symbolize a series of historical empires. But in the Similitudes of Enoch the figure is understood as a single person, a kind of heavenly Messiah who will be revealed on the day of judgment. Great disagreement prevails regarding the dating of the Similitudes. Originally they did not belong together with the other sections of 1 Enoch, which were composed during the second century B.C. The Similitudes are known exclusively from an Ethiopic translation as part of the Enoch apocalypse which was included in the canon of the Ethiopic church. Some believe that the document is of sectarian Christian origin. In support of that view is the fact that it was included in a Christian edition of the Bible and that it lacks pronounced features of non-Christian, Jewish influence. Most scholars think that the Similitudes must be Jewish, particularly because the Son of man has no features reminiscent of Jesus and, moreover (according to the usual view), is actually identified in 1 Enoch 71 with the patriarch Enoch, whom God had taken to himself, according to Gen. 5:24. In my view, what makes it impossible to use the Similitudes as a source for Palestinian Judaism contemporaneous with Jesus is that they contain ideas which are not otherwise attested, and particularly that no obvious citations or allusions appear in Christian or Jewish literature which show that the writing was known at that time. With regard to the other sections of 1 Enoch, there are many references both in Jewish and Christian writings, and they are also known from fragments of Aramaic and Greek versions.

We often have problems that stem from the fact that Jewish writings are preserved only in Christian copies, where the text has been adapted to a Christian interpretation. Perhaps the most complex example is the Testaments of the Twelve Patriarchs. The basic text can perhaps date from ca. 200 B.C., and contained no apocalyptic elements; all of the preserved manuscripts in Greek, Armenian, and other languages, however, are strongly stamped by later Jewish additions and Christian rewriting. There are traces of a long Jewish history of tradition which has modified the character of the document from a purely hortative composition for edification to a complex literary work where prophetic and apocalyptic elements play an important part. For us it is the many messianic prophecies which are interesting, but precisely these contain Christian editorial modifications (in several revisions), and in some instances it is quite impossible to decide how much is of pre-Christian origin.

There is a large body of Jewish literature in which we have relatively few problems with Christian interpolations. This includes the Old Testament Apocrypha and authors like Philo and Josephus. Through the comparatively recent discovery at the Dead Sea we have become acquainted with the library of the Qumran community, which, among other things, contains an abundance of original compositions from ca. 130 B.C. until ca. A.D. 70. This literature was esoteric. Very little of it ever emerged from the monastic community, even if some achieved some circulation among the Essenes (particularly the Damascus Document). It is possible that individual Essenes joined Christian communities. Thus one can perhaps find an explanation for the fact that the Johannine literature has a special quality reminiscent of typical writings from Qumran. But in the New Testament the Essenes are never mentioned by name, nor under other names (the designation "Essenes" is not found at Qumran, but rather such designations as "people of the new covenant," "the congregation of the saints," and many others, some of which are also used by Christians, like "the saints," "the elect," "sons of light," "the poor," and others). It is highly unlikely that Jesus, Paul, Luke, and so on, were acquainted with Qumran writings. This literature is frequently regarded as sectarian, particularly by Jewish scholars, and therefore uncharacteristic of the early Judaism of Jesus' day. But "sectarian" does not by itself imply "peripheral." We know that the Qumran community was dominated by priests who were intensely occupied by theological work, and there is a great deal to be said for the hypothesis that the leader in the earliest period, the "teacher of righteousness" (or, "the right teacher"), was simply the legitimate high priest who had been driven from Jerusalem in 153 B.C. by Jonathan, the Maccabean leader. That explains, among other things, the enormous self-confidence which is expressed in a series of psalms, of which he is the probable author. It is reasonable to assume that this rigorous, austere, law-abiding, and conservative community would retain ideas and customs from the priestly traditions of Jerusalem, and that their distinctive features by no means appeared so unusual and strange in the eyes of contemporary Jews as we may easily imagine. It is also worth mentioning that both

Josephus and Philo described the Essenes with respect and admiration. We cannot without reservation consider the Essenes and the Qumran community as identical, but probability suggests that the Essenes joined the legitimate high priest and that the learned priests at Qumran became the spiritual leaders of the Essenes. The name of the sect is derived from the Aramaic word corresponding to the Hebrew term *hasidim,* "the pious," which occurs in 1 Maccabees as a designation for the Jewish zealots for the Law who strongly opposed Hellenization and especially the attempt of Antiochus IV to abolish the distinctive customs of the Jews. From these *hasidim* both the Essenes and Pharisees originated, and they constituted the original crack troops in the rebel forces of Judas Maccabeus. It is not completely inconceivable that the name "Pharisees" originally might have been a nickname coined by the Essenes with the meaning "the seceders." In any event it is clear that the pious were divided because of different attitudes toward Maccabean politics, particularly Jonathan's coup, which installed a man as high priest who had not belonged to the priestly families which had a monopoly on the highest religious offices. It is reasonable to assume that the Essenes to a greater degree had preserved the attitudes and ideas of the old *hasidim* than the Pharisees. That gives Qumran a central and important place in Jewish cultural history.

At the time of Jesus, the Qumran community appeared to be a sect, an isolated community of "the saints of the last days," in some respects an interesting parallel phenomenon to the early Christian community, but with very little contact with people generally and without influence on cultural trends. The Essene literature therefore witnesses to special conceptions, some of which had ancient, genuinely Jewish roots. It was the Pharisees who were the dominant religious movement at the time of Jesus, and it is easy to believe that most of the literature which circulated in the last period before the time of Jesus was written by Pharisaic scribes and teachers of wisdom. But we can rarely decide with certainty whether a document actually represents Pharisaic perspectives. The most important case in this connection is the Psalms of Solomon, a collection of psalms from the middle of the first century B.C., at the beginning of the Roman occupation. It is not improbable that Pharisaic wisdom teachers stand behind most of the literature influenced by apocalypticism, in spite of the fact that the rabbis later took a position against all apocalyptic speculation. What we do not know is whether the apocalypses are armchair productions which represent the fantasies of an individual, or whether they reflect a more extensive communal setting. The beginning of apocalyptic goes at least back to the Hellenistic period, when the traditions of the prophets were studied as Holy Scripture with hidden significance, and interpreted as enigmatic warnings about imminent eschatological events. The book of Daniel, which originated ca. 165 B.C., can be understood as an edifying piece of propaganda in the desperate spiritual struggles of the pious. In this case we know that an apocalypse attained enormous popularity and exerted a strong influence among Essenes and Pharisees as well as among ordinary laypersons. We know very little about the broad effects of the later, much more speculative apocalyptic. Some apocalyptic ideas had become generally accepted by the time of Jesus (even if the Sadducean priestly party still opposed them). The result was that some of these ideas, such as the belief in the resurrection and final judgment, were no longer perceived as "apocalyptic."

3

The Historical Background

Jesus was a child of his time and can only be understood against the background of the circumstances and conceptions current in the Palestine of his day. But the problem of historical background is particularly complicated when it comes to Judaism, since for Jews religion and history are inextricably linked. It could hardly have been otherwise, since the basic religious conviction of Judaism is that Yahweh, the one true God, the creator of the universe and Lord of history, is the God of Israel, and Israel is God's elect people. This means that the entire history of Israel—especially as reflected in Scripture—must always be considered part of the religious background of whatever period is under consideration. Prior history lives on in the religion, contemporary history must be understood in the light of the religion, and the hope of religion includes the final goal for all history. The pedagogical purpose of the religious instruction of Judaism was to enable all Jews to feel as if they themselves had actually experienced the exodus from Egypt, the wandering in the desert, and the conquest of the holy land. To a considerable extent, the religious festivals consisted of a present cultic realization of saving historical events of the past. For these reasons, it is indeed impossible to depict the historical background of Jesus without including the whole sweep of biblical history, in addition to the actual conditions of that particular historical period. But, of course, that is virtually impossible. The history of ancient Israel—in the form of Scripture—can only be considered as part of the historical background of Jesus. There are, however, individual lines of inquiry which must be pursued much further back than might normally be the case when outlining the historical and cultural setting.

Babylon was the birthplace of Judaism. After 587 B.C., Jerusalem and the temple lay in ruins. Virtually the entire social and cultural upper crust had either been exterminated or deported to Babylon, and foreign immigrants took over the ownerless land. The exiles succeeded in holding themselves together and protecting their identity through religion. Without the temple as a rallying point, a new center had to be secured and that was achieved through the tradition which had become fixed in Scripture. The written Law became the unassailable authority, and through the commands of the Law Judaism was both defined and characterized. Those traditionally Jewish customs which separated them from other people were given special emphasis (e.g., circumcision, Sabbath observance, regulations for pure and impure food, and so on). Synagogues arose as religious and social gathering places. In the synagogue Judaism received its form and Jews found their identity. The remnants of the nation of Israel became a cultic community. Helped by the story of the miraculous redemption from Egypt and by prophetic visions, the community held fast to the hope of liberation and a bright future in a restored Jerusalem. This expectation received some basis in reality when the Babylonian Empire began to crumble and the unknown prophet who stands behind Isaiah 40–55—Deutero-Isaiah, or Second Isaiah, as he is called—greeted Cyrus as a savior sent from Yahweh and wrote poetry inspired by the words and images of the festival liturgies about the miraculous transformation which was about to take place.

The reality turned out to be much less spectacular than expected. The Jews did receive permission to return to their homeland and restore the temple. But the actual conditions there put an end to all optimistic expectations. Prophets such as Haggai and Zechariah did their best to encourage the little flock, which soon encountered suspicion and opposition on the part of their new neighbors. The hope which they had at first placed in Zerubbabel, a descendant of David, died out—for reasons which are now obscure. When a new temple was eventually consecrated in 516 B.C., the older people, who knew something of how magnificent the temple of Solomon had been, could only weep. Thanks to strong leaders like Nehemiah and Ezra, together with new groups who returned home from Babylon, Jerusalem succeeded in becoming a Jewish temple-city where the commandments of the Law of Moses were carried out rigorously. But clashes with others who lived in the land (*'am haaretz*, "people of the land"), who were for the most part of Israelite descent though intermarried with foreign immigrants, became intensified. The eventual result was a permanent religious schism, with the Samaritans setting up their own temple on Gerizim.

The small, impoverished province of Judea occupied a privileged position in the Persian Empire because of the temple. For the great majority of Jewish believers who lived outside of Palestine, Jerusalem, with its temple, was a religious symbol, a spiritual capital. This situation changed little after Alexander had crushed the Persian Empire. The high priest, who presided over the Sanhedrin, was in every respect the chief representative of the Jewish temple community. The dream of the restoration of Israel as a state under a new David appeared increasingly utopian. We actually have little concrete historical information about the internal conditions between ca. 400 B.C. (the time of Ezra) and 200 B.C., when the control of Palestine went over from the Ptolemaic dynasty of Egypt to the Seleucids of Syria. Judaism must have experienced a period of growth. Adherents to the Jewish faith were found everywhere. In particular cities, especially in Alexandria, they formed exclusively Jewish settlements. Jewish wisdom poetry flourished; both classical and contemporary Jewish literature appeared in Greek dress. But Hellenistic culture was also very influential in Palestine itself. Even among the priests in Jerusalem, Greek customs forced their way in, and there was a very strong tendency toward both a liberalization and a spiritualization of Judaism. Some simply dreamed of turning the ethical monotheism of Judaism into a universal religion. There was, however, a conservative protest against Hellenization, and circles of pious zealots for the Law fought to preserve traditional Jewish identity.

The dramatic turning point came when Antiochus IV, with the active collaboration of priests in Jerusalem, attempted by force to eradicate the more orthodox, exclusivistic form of Judaism. He forbade circumcision and Sabbath observance, erected a statue of Zeus in the temple and sent messages around to all cities and villages to the effect that Jews be compelled to do what for them could only be considered idolatry. He accomplished the exact opposite of his intentions. The *hasidim* ("pious ones") rose in revolt in a holy war under the leadership of the Maccabees. After a five-year struggle, Judas Maccabeus, in the winter of 164 B.C., was able to purify and rededicate the desecrated temple. A new epoch in the history of Judaism began. The conscious Hellenization and universalization of the Jewish religion came to an abrupt halt. From now on, Judaism became the practice of the Mosaic Law. Yet even though the fanatical zealots of the Law had been triumphant, religious harmony did not result. The development of factional groups then began in earnest. Here again a close connection between history and religion manifests itself. The party factions expressed different responses to Maccabean (Hasmonean) politics. An important consequence of the successful rebellion was that the narrow boundaries of the temple community were shattered. There arose a Jewish state which at its greatest extent was virtually coextensive with the ancient kingdom of David. Galilee was incorporated into Judea and its inhabitants forcibly circumcised ca. 100 B.C. That sounds surprising, since, during the Roman occupation, Galilee was the center of nationalistic and fanatical religious unrest, and it was from Galilee that many of the Zealots were recruited.

It is easy to understand how these violent events, which gave Jews some measure of freedom and independence for the first time since the deportation to Babylon, began to encourage dreams for the future and revive messianic ideas. Yet there are only weak and problematic indications of attempts by the Hasmonean princes (or their adherents)—who temporarily unified in one person both the political-military and the highest religious authority—to exploit the messianic prophecies for their own advantage. It is easier to demonstrate that these were used by their opponents. The Essenes refused to acknowledge a Maccabean high priest and regarded it as objectionable that temporal and spiritual authority were vested in the same individual. The Pharisees protested against the use of the title "king," because it was reserved for the Davidic house. But the real outbreak of general, popular messianic expectations occurred only after freedom was lost once again when the Romans took control in 63 B.C.

The Roman vassal King Herod (37–4 B.C.), who came from Idumea, which had also been conquered by the Hasmoneans and on whose populace circumcision and the Law had been forced, vainly attempted to win over the hearts of the Jews to himself by building a magnificent temple. Some pious fanatics found it easier to put up with a foreign temporal ruler forced on them than with a Jewish one. Their ideal was not that Israel should rise as a state like other states, but that it should be a holy theocracy. Qumran lay in ruins after an earthquake during most of the reign of Herod the Great, yet, strangely enough, it appears that the Essenes gained the favor of the king. It is even possible that they had their center in a section of the capital city itself.

When Herod died in 4 B.C., the administration was divided among his four sons. Herod Antipas, widely known from the story of John the Baptist and Jesus, received Galilee and Perea (the region east of the Jordan, with the exception of the Decapolis, an association of independent Hellenistic cities). Archelaus in Judea behaved so irresponsibly that the Romans replaced him after 10 years and installed a Roman provincial governor. At the same time they decreed a tax levy which was the primary cause why Judas the Galilean, from Gamala, organized a band of Zealot guerillas with the motto "We have no other king than God!" Josephus describes a number of other revolutionary leaders at that time and maintains that many of them called themselves "king."

4

John the Baptist

Josephus describes three or four religious "schools" which were influential at the time of Jesus. He describes the *Essenes* in greatest detail, probably because they were the least known and seemed the most fascinating to Hellenistic readers. The *Pharisees* were the largest party, and had a strong influence within the institution of the synagogue. The *Sadducees* were an aristocratic, conservative priestly party. Josephus also describes the anarchists surrounding Judas, who ideologically had a great deal in common with the Pharisees. However, they differentiated themselves from them by refusing to pay taxes to Caesar. Josephus does not actually mention the activity of the *Zealots* during the time of Pilate. They appear again several years later, only to play a fateful role before and during the Jewish revolt. No one has tried to connect Jesus to the Sadducees, though some scholars have regarded him as an Essene, a Pharisee, or a Zealot. This demonstrates the difficulty of mapping the religious terrain. Most people belonged to no party whatever, even if in some critical situations of conflict it could happen that they were compelled to choose one side or the other. Particularly the triumphal entry into Jerusalem together with the purification of the temple and the saying about selling one's coat in order to buy a sword form the basis for believing that Jesus actually represented the revolutionary, Zealot line (one of the disciples even bore the appellation "the Zealot"). But even these features are difficult to understand on the basis of such a presupposition. Why did not the soldiers intervene? Why were none of Jesus' adherents apprehended? The possibility should not be ignored that some could well have pinned their hopes on the chance that Jesus might become a revolutionary leader (cf. John 6:15). Yet there is nothing in Jesus' preaching to indicate his support for a Zealot program.

There is scarcely any better reason for making Jesus into an Essene, even if the designation is used fairly generally and not necessarily connected with the elite group at Qumran. Common to all Essenes was the rigorous, pedantic observation of the demands of the Law, particularly in matters relating to Sabbath observance and ritual purity. Essene circles would not have accepted a person who feasted with tax collectors and other objectionable types.

Despite Jesus' blunt attacks against the scribes, it is easier to see how some Jewish scholars can actually regard Jesus as representing a type of Pharisaism. The famous sages Hillel and Shammai were both Pharisees, but they were often at odds in their interpretation of the Torah. So perhaps we too should consider the possibility that Jesus might have been a rabbi. Yet here we come to a problematic point: Jesus did not teach at all like the scribes. They were pedantic teachers in the art of interpreting the Law. Jesus was a popular preacher with a prophetic message.

There was, however, another movement in Palestine at the time of Jesus and one which was certainly important for him. Aside from the crucifixion, the most secure historical fact about Jesus is that he was one of those who came to John the Baptist to be baptized. John was the only person we know who had a decisive influence on Jesus' religious development. Jesus called him the greatest person who had ever lived (Matt. 11:11). The evangelists begin their narratives by telling about John. The same is true of some of the summary reports of the proclamation of the apostles in Acts (1:22; 10:37; 13:24f.; cf. 1:5; 11:16; 19:4). In Luke 1–2, reports about the miraculous births of John and Jesus are woven together to form a unity, and they are made close relatives. John is thus accorded a place and function as near as possible to Jesus in the history of salvation.

John clearly stands in the shadow of Jesus, even though it is because of the Gospels that he was not forgotten like so many others (e.g., Bannus, who had the young Josephus as his disciple). The situation is somewhat paradoxical. The same sources that emphasize his greatness and monumental contribution have little specific information permitting us to realize his importance. On the one hand, we could suppose that here by accident one of many obscure figures has emerged and been given a reputation because of a disciple's fame. On the other hand, it is also possible that an extremely important teacher has been reduced to a vague background figure, simply because all attention has come to be focused on his successor. When reading Josephus, one gets the impression that the latter possibility was the case, since he does not have much to say about Jesus (not even considering the interpolations which a Christian copyist made in *Antiquities* 18.63-64). Josephus himself wrote little more than that Jesus was a man who lived in an exemplary manner and was known for his noble morals. Yet he devotes a lengthy section to John the Baptist (*Antiquities* 18.116-119). Josephus reports that many thought that the humiliating defeat Herod Antipas suffered by the Arabian king Aretas was God's punishment for the sin he had committed by taking the life of John, who "was a good man and had exhorted the Jews to lead righteous lives, to practice justice towards their fellows and piety towards God, and so doing to join in baptism." Josephus continues: "In his view this was a necessary preliminary if baptism was to be acceptable to God. They must not employ it to gain pardon for whatever sins they committed, but as a consecration of the body implying that the soul was already thoroughly cleansed by right behaviour" (*Antiquities* 18.117; trans. L. Feldman, LCL). As the real reason why Herod allowed John to be executed, Josephus reports that the king feared that the Baptist's influence over people was so strong that he could get them to do whatever he wanted, even to participate in a rebellion, if such a thing should occur to him. The historian betrays no knowledge of the macabre story in Mark 6:17-29.

When Josephus depicts the Baptist as a preacher of virtue with the motto "a sound soul in a sound body," it is certainly a distortion designed for Greco-Roman tastes. What he says about John's remarkable ability to influence the masses, however, is fascinating. A more satisfying perspective is found in the portrait of him in the

Gospels. As a prophet of judgment and a preacher of repentance, he persuaded people of the imminence of the day of judgment and that it was necessary to protect themselves from punishment by confessing their sins and receiving the forgiveness of sins in baptism and dedicating themselves to live so as not to incur new guilt.

Many scholars have connected John with the Essenes, but there is really no valid basis for such a view. John lived a celibate life outside of civilization, nourishing himself with simple food from wild plants and wearing a minimum of clothing, characteristics associated with ancient "holy men." He probably followed the pattern found in ancient prophetic traditions (cf. 2 Kings 1:8; what is here said about Elijah could have been secondarily applied to John). The evidence is meager and burdened with considerable uncertainty because it is shaped by the Christian conception of the Baptist as a prophetic forerunner of the Messiah, as the eschatological manifestation of Elijah predicted in the final statement in the last of the ancient prophetic books (Mal. 3:1; 4:5f.).

The special baptismal ritual he practiced and the significance attached to his baptism has placed John in a unique position and given him the appellation "the Baptist." Cultic purification rituals are universal. A special purification, or baptism, providing initiation into a religious community is a natural ritual when all those outside of the community are considered impure. But the baptism of John was unique and must be assigned a particular significance. Perhaps the most striking feature was the Baptist's active role. It was he himself who baptized (through pouring or immersion) those who came. That certainly implies that baptism must be understood as a sacramental act. The one baptized received something from God through baptism, and that something must be the forgiveness of sins. People were baptized following the confession of sin, which indicates that a promise of the forgiveness of sins was connected with the baptismal ritual. It is striking that later Christian baptism and the baptism of John can be characterized in exactly the same way, as a baptism for the forgiveness of sins (Mark 1:4; Acts 2:38; etc.). If the difference between Johannine and Christian baptism is to be stressed, it is always pointed out that only Christian baptism gives a share in the Holy Spirit. Christian baptism is a baptism with water and the Spirit, while John only baptized with water (Mark 1:8; Matt. 3:11; Luke 3:16; John 1:26, 31, 33; 3:5, 8; Acts 1:5; 11:16; 19:1-7). A second feature peculiar to John is that he did not utilize baptism to form a community. Baptism did not function as an admission ticket into a group. All the same, baptism was a once-and-for-all phenomenon and consequently essentially different from the daily purifications at Qumran or the cultic purifications for removing ritual impurity as prescribed by the Law of Moses. John baptized all who fulfilled the given conditions: that they repent of their sins and promise to avoid committing new ones (without making it necessary to imagine an idea of absolute sinlessness). The third decisive aspect is the eschatological orientation. Baptism is clearly an eschatological sacrament, not only something which can occur but once in a person's life, but a unique opportunity in all of human history as well. It is in these last days, just before the Judge takes his place on the seat of judgment, that the baptism of repentance for the forgiveness of sins is offered as a possibility of salvation. For all who heard his message, John probably preached baptism as the final opportunity to be saved. It is unnecessary to conclude that only those baptized by him could be included in the remnant of Israel who will be spared judgment. (It is, for example, conceivable that John accepted the Essenes as they were.)

Baptism was the positive element in the Baptist's preaching. Otherwise he appears to have placed all emphasis upon the imminent judgment which provided a motivation for repentance. Unlike the classical prophets of judgment who prophesied God's collective punishment of the people, what is reported of John's preaching suggests an individual appeal for personal responsibility. It is striking that Matt. 3:2 summarizes the Baptist's call for repentance in the same manner as Jesus' gospel (4:17): "Repent, for the kingdom of heaven is at hand." In the preaching of Jesus, the kingdom of God is primarily a positive conception. The fact that it is near is a message of joy. There is nothing reported about John in the first three Gospels which can satisfactorily explain why Matt. 3:2 makes him a herald of the kingdom of God. Even Matthew depicts him as a rigorous prophet of the day of judgment. For John it is the *wrath* of God which comes, not the kingdom of God (Matt. 3:7). While individuals can be saved from the wrath of judgment through repentance and baptism, nothing suggests that John thought of a restoration for Israel. Sayings to the effect that God can raise up children for Abraham from the stones in the field (Matt. 3:9) pull the rug out from under the entire doctrine of the exclusive election of Israel.

Of particular interest are the more specific indications about what John thought would happen, particularly the fact that he saw a connection between his own ministry and that of the one who would come after him. That one is so much greater that John is unworthy to be the slave who loosens the thongs of his sandals. He will not baptize with water, but with fire. In other words, he is the one who shall carry out the final judgment. As the farmer after the threshing gathers the grain into the barn and burns up the husks and chaff, so shall he who comes separate out the worthy and take care of them, but destroy the unworthy (Mark 1:7f.; Matt. 3:11f.; Luke 3:16f.). To whom does John refer? For the evangelists it is clear that John is pointing to Jesus, who is to be the Messiah. The evangelists regarded John as the forerunner of Christ, the one who prepared a way for him (Mark 1:2f.; Matt. 11:10; Luke 7:27). It is conceivable that prophecies about the stronger one who shall come were shaped by the idea of a forerunner and placed on the lips of John the Baptist in Christian tradition. But would the predictions take on such a form? In John 1:19-27 we have a perfect example of a Christian adaptation of traditions about the Baptist which turns him into a completely unambiguous witness to Jesus. Yet the formulations in the synoptic Gospels are not likely to encourage anyone to think particularly of the earthly Jesus. Mark 1:7f. is perhaps the least objectionable passage. Nothing there is said of the role of judgment, but just that he who shall come will baptize, not with water, but with the Holy Spirit. Matthew 3:11 and Luke 3:16 report that he will baptize with the Holy Spirit and fire. That causes us to think of the miracle on the day of Pentecost (Acts 2:3-4), even though the fire mentioned in the following verses (Acts 2:19-21) symbolizes the judgment of God. In this case it is likely that a secondary adaptation has been made and that originally the Baptist spoke only of fire. His successor is he who will unhesitatingly accomplish the judgment of God. John cannot be referring to God himself, although that would be in keeping with Malachi 3–4, to which this saying refers. That would make the comparison with the unworthy John ridiculous and the anthropomorphism (God's shoelace) too ludicrous. He must (if the saying is genuine) have anticipated a human figure, but one who would eclipse his prophet more than a king his servant. But if John referred to the Messiah, and that is certainly the most obvious conclusion, it is striking that the only messianic function mentioned is the purgation of the unworthy. This motif replaces that of the traditional messianic judgment of the pagans.

On the basis of such fragmentary evidence, it would be rash to attempt to delineate the eschatological perspective of John in any more detail. We would certainly prefer to know more, since it is likely that Jesus himself, at the time of his baptism, accepted the views of John in all essentials. Whether Jesus himself once belonged to the circle of John's disciples and played a prominent role there is not easy to determine. There are indications which point in that direction. Mark 1:14 and Matt. 4:12 say that it was not until John was thrown into prison that Jesus returned to Galilee and began his preaching ministry. In that case it was during his imprisonment that John learned of the remarkable things Jesus did, and began to wonder whether perhaps Jesus was "he who shall come" (Luke 7:18-23; Matt. 11:1-6). We must disregard Matt. 3:14, which presupposes that John knew that Jesus was the Messiah even before he was baptized. In John 3:22-26 and 4:1 the assertion is made that Jesus began his ministry in competition with John and with his own corresponding ministry of baptism. It would be easier to understand the origins of Christian baptism if Jesus himself had performed baptisms. But the absolute silence of the first three evangelists compels us to suppose that Jesus did not continue John's ministry of baptism. Was baptism so closely connected to the person of John that it stopped when he was imprisoned? Or did Jesus have fundamental reasons for avoiding a ministry of baptism? We can with certainty claim little more than that the practice of baptism would not have been discontinued unless Jesus regarded it as unnecessary. Practical difficulties cannot provide an adequate explanation. On the other hand, there is no basis for thinking that there was a breach between Jesus and John, even if Jesus went his own way and in many respects his proclamation differed from that of his teacher. But just as Paul could later write, "For Christ did not send me to baptize but to preach the gospel" (1 Cor. 1:17), Jesus must also have thought that God did not send him to baptize but to preach the gospel. Yet, this expressed or implied opposition between baptism and the proclamation of the gospel is quite remarkable. For John, baptism was a form of "gospel." The discussion about authority in Mark 11:27-33 (and par.) presupposes that the baptism of John was "from heaven" and therefore divinely inspired. Matthew 21:32 and

Luke 7:29f. clearly indicate that those who did not submit to John's baptism were refusing God's offer of mercy. Since it would have been unnatural for the later Christian community to use such strong terms, it is probable that they represent the views of Jesus.

Why did Jesus not continue where John left off? There appear to be two possible explanations. First, the special offer of mercy was linked to John and was withdrawn when he was out of the picture. Second, baptism was no longer necessary because Jesus could offer something better. Since it is a fact that Jesus offered salvation to more than those whom John had baptized, the last explanation is probably correct. Yet it is both historically and psychologically natural that the arrest of John itself led to an interruption of the practice of baptism, in view of its dependence on his person. But what did Jesus have to offer that made baptism superfluous? The problem must remain open until later in our study. First we must examine more closely the relationship between Jesus and John and the consequence of the fact that they appeared at very nearly the same time.

In the Christian community, the evaluation of John must have been problematic. Not all of John's disciples sided with Jesus. That means that for some of them John was a greater prophet than Jesus. Their veneration of John and his teaching hindered them from completely accepting Jesus. This seems to exclude the possibility that John could have pointed to Jesus as his successor, as the one he expected as the eschatological judge. At the most, one can imagine that what he heard about Jesus while he sat in prison kindled a certain hope regarding him. To depict John merely as the messianic forerunner of Jesus could therefore not be easy. The fact that the Gospel accounts of John are in general unpolemical and positive can be explained only if it was an incontestable fact that Jesus had been baptized by John and that Jesus himself had expressed his unqualified acceptance of him. Along with these historical arguments is the important observation that Jewish eschatological expectations could easily accommodate *both* individuals. They could be categorized in mutually complementary eschatological roles. If Jesus was the Messiah, then John was Elijah. To proclaim John as Elijah made it that much easier to believe that Jesus was the Messiah. The baptism of Jesus could be fitted into this scenario. There were certain obvious difficulties in accounting for the fact that Jesus allowed himself to be baptized by John. In the first instance, this gave John an apparently primary position; second, since baptism would bestow the forgiveness of sins it could be inferred that even Jesus was conscious of having sinned. The difficulty is clearly reflected in Matt. 3:13-17, where John himself says that it would have been more appropriate that Jesus baptize him. In the apocryphal Gospel of the Hebrews there is a fictional dialog between Jesus and his disciples. They recommend that everyone should go to John for baptism. Jesus responds (trans. M. R. James, *The Apocryphal New Testament* [Oxford: Clarendon, 1924], p. 6): "Wherein have I sinned, that I should go and be baptized of him? Unless peradventure this very thing which I have said is a sin of ignorance." The Gospel of John mentions Jesus' baptism only indirectly (1:32-34). For the most part, the problem is solved by giving the baptism of Jesus a special meaning. The emphasis is placed on the miraculous revelation which occurred in connection with Jesus' baptism. The Holy Spirit descended on Jesus and God proclaimed him as his Son (Mark 1:10f. and par.; John 1:29-34). Matthew and John have a tendency to let the miracle and the heavenly voice function as a revelation and proclamation to others, assuming that Jesus was certainly God's Son previously, and that he knew who he was. Yet we are primarily dealing here with the *report of a call,* akin to those narrated about several Old Testament prophets. Yet this account is distinctive, because Jesus was not just called to be a prophet but was called and anointed to be the Messiah (cf. Isa. 42:1; 61:1; Ps. 2:7). After the baptism, Jesus was led by the Spirit out into the desert to be tested and show himself worthy of his calling.

Even though we are dealing with a legendary story replete with symbolism, it is likely to suppose that his baptism, because it is the only concrete event of which we have knowledge, was for Jesus a religious experience which he understood as a divine calling or election. It can be said more truly for Jesus than for all the others who have experienced baptism as the turning point in their lives that it *began with baptism.* From then on everything was completely changed. From then on he was under the direction of the Spirit. His life was no longer his own, but was guided by a higher destiny. His separation from John had already begun at this point, even though it is possible that he for some time was counted among John's disciples.

Since the assessment of John expressed in several sayings of Jesus not only reveals admiration for him personally, but also reflects a particular theological interpretation which has implications for his self-understanding, we shall return to this subject in another context. The question of what John thought of himself, whether he identified himself with any particular eschatological role, is difficult to answer definitively. John 1:19-23 is an ideal scene which represents the evangelist's perspective. The fact that John, unlike the other evangelists, does not identify John with Elijah is certainly one indication that the evangelist regarded Jesus alone as the fulfillment of all eschatological expectations. In his own person he combined the roles of Elijah, the Prophet, and the Messiah. Yet it may be historically correct that John wanted only to be an anonymous voice, a warning cry before the final judgment. It is possible that he understood himself more as a preacher of repentance than as a prophet of judgment. Yet the introduction of baptism as a nearly sacramental act nonetheless is evidence for a consciousness of a vocation which must be regarded as virtually prophetic in character. And since he preached judgment as imminent, the unavoidable conclusion is that he must have regarded himself as the last prophet of God. The only one who could come after him was the Messiah.

It is now appropriate to attempt to provide a survey of the variety of eschatological roles current at that time.

5

Roles in the Eschatological Drama

Eschatology, narrowly defined as "teaching about the last things," presupposes a dualistic conception of two worlds which succeed one another. The present world will come to an end and be replaced by a new one. A qualitative opposition is thought to exist between these two worlds. The new state of existence will be perfect in all respects, while the old world is both evil and unhappy. Consequently, its destruction is uniformly understood in terms of *judgment*. In early Jewish and Christian apocalyptic we sometimes find a consistent and universal type of eschatology which literally implies that all creation will be destroyed and that God will create a new heaven and a new earth. That in this connection foreign ideas and motifs from Persian and Greek mythology and cosmology were borrowed can easily be demonstrated. These notions were combined with earlier Israelite conceptions of a more limited future upheaval, where the central emphasis is on the reversal of Israel's fortune. At that point in time, Israel had a wretched and disgraceful existence under the domination of ungodly people. Eventually the nation would experience God's intervention, with the punishment of the oppressors and God's bestowal of the kingdom, power, and glory to the elect. Even though we are dealing with conceptions which are not logically compatible, they are woven together in such a way that they are inseparable and it can be difficult to determine which idea is predominant. We can venture to suggest, however, that what consistently gives eschatology its pathos is the thought of salvation, the restoration of the elect. But such vague modes of expression leave further questions open: who are the elect, and what does salvation involve? Does it concern the 12 tribes of Israel, the kingdom of David, the small remnant of the faithful or the souls of the righteous? Does it imply a this-worldly restoration or a heavenly state of blessedness?

We can safely say that it is not only modern scholars who find it difficult to grasp the individual threads and separate them from each other. The eschatological views of Judaism were relatively indefinite and full of internal contradictions. Perhaps we think that it ought at least to be possible to use one simple criterion to determine whether we are dealing with a this-worldly, immanent (and relative) eschatology or with a transcendent, otherworldly one, namely, whether it involves a resurrection of the dead. Yet even this distinction does not work. It is possible, for instance, to hold that some of the deceased will rise again to new life in order to be present and experience happiness together with the generation of Jews living when the glorious kingdom is established on the earth.

To make this more concrete, it might be helpful to consider two texts from about the same period. They are interesting because they clearly represent a scholastic attempt systematically to combine the older, more limited, and originally nationalistic "eschatology" with later conceptions of a complete cosmic upheaval. According to 4 Ezra 7:26-36 (RSV, 2 Esdras):

> For behold, the time will come, when the signs which I have foretold to you will come to pass, that the city which now is not seen shall appear, and the land which now is hidden shall be disclosed. And every one who has been delivered from the evils that I have foretold shall see my wonders. For my son the Messiah shall be revealed with

those who are with him, and those who remain shall rejoice four hundred years. And after these years my son the Messiah shall die, and all who draw human breath. And the world shall be turned back to primeval silence for seven days, as it was at the first beginnings; so that no one shall be left. And after seven days the world, which is not yet awake, shall be roused, and that which is corruptible shall perish. And the earth shall give up those who are asleep in it, and the dust those who dwell silently in it; and the chambers shall give up the souls which have been committed to them. And the Most High shall be revealed upon the seat of judgment, and compassion shall pass away, and patience shall be withdrawn; but only judgment shall remain, truth shall stand, and faithfulness shall grow strong. And recompense shall follow, and the reward shall be manifested; righteous deeds shall awake, and unrighteous deeds shall not sleep. Then the pit of torment shall appear, and opposite it shall be the place of rest; and the furnace of hell shall be disclosed, and opposite it the paradise of delight.

Some of the same motifs occur also in Revelation 20. Yet since the text is a bit long and easily accessible, we provide only a summary: An angel will descend from heaven and bind Satan and confine him to the bottomless pit for a thousand years. When they are completed, he will be released for a short period. During these one thousand years Christ will reign together with the martyrs who have been resurrected to new life. When Satan is again released, he will assemble people without number from the four corners of the earth and lead them to battle against the saints. But they will be consumed with fire from heaven and the devil will be cast into the lake of fire for eternal torment. Judgment follows immediately thereafter. The earth and the heavens disappear. All the dead arise and are judged according to their deeds. Those whose names are not written in the book of life are cast into the lake of fire. A new heaven and a new earth are then created, and the new Jerusalem descends from heaven and God makes his dwelling among humans.

In both of these texts a combination of old and new eschatology occurs, insofar as we find a doubling of the themes of judgment and salvation in order to accommodate the messianic kingdom, which turns out to be a provisional state of happiness for the few. This doubling is particularly striking in the Revelation of John, where we have two wars (19:11-21 and 20:7-10), two triumphs over Satan, two judgment scenes, two resurrections, two states of blessedness. When we read further in the description of the new Jerusalem and the newly created paradise, we get the clear impression that even though the Messiah, the Lamb, is mentioned, he has no real function. In 4 Ezra also the Messiah naturally belongs to those who are resurrected to eternal life in the new world, but he is not so much as mentioned in that context. The Messiah belongs to the last phase of the old world.

A trace of this trend of thought is also found in Paul in 1 Cor. 15:23-25. Here it is mentioned that all will be resurrected in due course; the first is Christ, then at his return all those who belong to Christ, and thereafter the rest (or, "then comes the end"), when he turns over royal authority to God the Father after having made an end to every rule, authority, and power. For he shall be king until he has placed all enemies under his feet (cf. Ps. 110:1). In the following verses we learn that the last enemy to be destroyed is death, and that finally the Son will subject himself to the one who placed all things under him, so that God will be all in all. It is not completely clear whether Paul also has in mind a resurrection for believers first and only then a universal resurrection (for judgment) later, or whether the last stage has completely disappeared. It is also unclear whether the dominion of Christ begins with the resurrection and lasts until the final enemy is conquered, or whether Paul also expects a thousand-year kingdom after the second coming of Jesus. But the most striking feature of all is the idea that the dominion of Christ is *provisional*. It lasts only as long as there are still hostile forces to conquer. When harmony is restored, the Messiah no longer has a necessary function. Then it is only God who prevails.

In one text in the Gospels there occurs the conception of the "kingdom of the Son of man," a kingdom which clearly is both this-worldly and provisional, as it is succeeded by the kingdom of the Father, where the righteous shall shine like the sun (Matt. 13:41-43; cf. Dan. 12:3). But here we are dealing with a secondary elaboration of a parable. We have no authentic tradition which proves that Jesus held eschatological conceptions involving a distinction between the kingdom of the Messiah and the kingdom of God. He speaks of the imminence and coming of the kingdom of God in such a way that no room is left for an intermediate messianic kingdom. If the Messiah will have any future function at all, it must be as a representative of God's kingdom and as the one through whom God rules. He is, as it were, the vicegerent of God. A remarkable saying, which is transmitted in two fairly divergent forms in Luke 22:29f. and Matt. 19:28 (and which will be discussed in a later chapter), mentions how the apostles will receive a share of the royal authority of the Son of man and rule over the 12 tribes of Israel. This reflects the Jewish expectation of a national restoration. On the other hand, there are sayings which link the expectation of salvation to the resurrection and eternal life in another state of existence.

In this chapter the Jewish background is the focus of our interest. It may appear methodologically suspect to draw on both Christian and Jewish texts. But the New Testament is not only an important source for Jewish conceptions; it is our surest guide for deciding which Jewish ideas and themes can be regarded as current in Jesus' environment. There is no point in producing material from Jewish texts if there is no indication in the New Testament (particularly within the Gospels and Acts) that it is relevant to the background of Jesus and the early church.

Our discussion is limited to the problem of the eschatological actors who are mentioned, that is, individuals who are expected to play a specific role in the eschatological drama. Of particular concern are those who could have provided a pattern for Jesus and with whom he might have identified himself. Since the unanimous testimony of the New Testament is that Jesus is the Messiah, it is obvious that messianic roles stand in the center of our interest. At the same time there is the problem of how Jesus could be identified as a Jewish Messiah. There are some indications that Jesus himself had reservations about such an identification, and many scholars firmly deny that he actually did regard himself as the Messiah. We must therefore consider as well the figures who either appear alongside of or in place of the Messiah in Jewish eschatology. More specifically, we must investigate the various conceptions of a final prophet. On the other hand, texts which feature Michael or other angelic figures as eschatological saviors do not require our attention. Nonetheless, it may also be necessary to consider conceptions which, though not directly found in an eschatological context, in one way or another could be indirectly relevant and perhaps provide a point of departure for identifying other possibilities. Specific examples include the servant of the Lord of Deutero-Isaiah and certain ideas about the righteous martyr in literature produced near the time of Jesus.

At the same time, it must be emphasized that in most conceptions of an eschatological upheaval, both in the Old Testament prophets and in the apocalypses, human activity plays virtually no role. It is *God* who judges and saves, and the new state of affairs which is established is the kingdom of *God* where *God* is omnipotent and the will of *God* prevails. If God crowns his work by installing a king on Zion, that king serves more as a symbol of God's faithfulness to his promises and goodwill toward Israel than as God's collaborator in the work of redemption. Jesus himself also spoke of judgment and salvation as acts of *God*. The function of the Son of man as judge is mentioned, but only in sayings of doubtful authenticity. The extent to which human actors played any role at all in Jesus' eschatological perspective remains an unsolved problem.

Yet one reservation should be quickly expressed. The fact that the texts do not mention human actors does not necessarily mean that there is no place for them. If apocalyptic literature speaks only of God's sovereign activity in judging and saving, it cannot be concluded that there was no room for a Messiah or that people did not participate, for example, in the holy war against forces hostile to God. It is also risky to reconstruct different sources for a document based on the fact that within it one can find some eschatological descriptions mentioning only God's activity, and other corresponding descriptions in which people play important roles. It is far from certain that the ancient authors were conscious of any tension between those two points of view. A comparison can be made between the way in which the saving events of the past are described in the classical literature of Israel. In cultic texts such as prayers and psalms, it is perfectly normal and stylistically appropriate to mention only how *God* with a mighty arm crushed the enemies of Israel and led the people to salvation and blessedness. But naturally one could also praise God for having sent Moses or Joshua or other leaders. In the royal psalms God and the king can alternately be accorded honor for the same great achievement. Since the king is both God's instrument and God's son, no contradiction is involved.

On the other hand, there is the possibility that a basic theocratic principle underlies apocalyptic thought, such that all human roles are ignored and eschatological salvation is ascribed to the activity of God alone. Therein may lie an implicit protest against activist programs which give credit to human leaders. Such notions, even if they are never really consistently worked out, can certainly be detected in the Holy Scriptures, from which Jewish eschatology derived its inspiration, both in the prophetic books and in the narratives of Israelite history. To have confidence in weapons, war horses, and a large army is presented partly as sin and partly as gross unbelief. All that is required is that Israel place its entire confidence in Yahweh and renounce all human security. Jeremiah was regarded as a defeatist and a traitor because he regarded foreign domination as God's way of punishing his sinful people, a punishment to which they must humbly submit so that, in time, the yoke might be removed at God's good pleasure. Probably in every period there were religious circles, often constituting an oppressed minority, who recommended simply waiting upon the Lord. Even in that normally implied political passivity, it must not be confused with pacifism, since the possibility was always present that God would summon them to a holy war. This is clearly illustrated at Qumran, where the distinctive, semiapocalyptic document "The War between the Sons of Light and the Sons of Darkness" (lQM), exhibits the sort of dreams about the future with which groups that were isolated and remote from the world could sustain themselves.

It is difficult to trace quietistic traditions down through history, for political events often create new situations which correspondingly alter religious attitudes and relationships. Examples are found in the Maccabean revolt and the Hasmonean monarchy. There are certainly lines connecting the *hasidim* ("pious ones") at the time of the Maccabees back to the time of Ezra and even further back to the first impoverished postexilic community. We can easily imagine that a quietistic attitude was prevalent among those who were able, by a miracle of God, to return to Jerusalem to rebuild the temple. Nehemiah taught the community to build with a sword at hand. Fertile soil for nationalistic and militaristic dreams, however, cannot have persisted throughout the entire long period before the Maccabean revolt. There is actually very little reliable information about Jewish history during this time. What information there is pertains to political events which occurred outside of the control of the Jewish community and without their being able to play an active role. In the religious and cultural area, however, a great deal occurred, precisely because Judaism found its identity in religious and cultural distinctiveness and to that end had freedom to develop and assert itself in those areas. We can naturally assume that the scribal preoccupation with the ancient history of Israel and the classical prophets could preserve the vision of a new David and a new people of Israel alike. It is even more understandable if we find, on the one hand, tendencies to define Judaism in a purely religious way as the only true cultic community, and, on the other hand, tendencies to pursue universal religious and moral wisdom and turn Judaism into the best exponent of it. The latter tendency corresponds to a factor easily overlooked, namely, that the vast majority of adherents to the Jewish faith lived outside of Palestine and were the loyal subjects of pagan nations. The spiritual climate varied with geography as well as with history.

The Messiah

The Gospels foster the impression that all Jews were intensely preoccupied with the coming of the Messiah. Here and there, to be sure, it is clear that it was actually only a minority of Jews "who were looking for the redemption of Jerusalem" (Luke 2:38). The situation was probably not much different from that known from church history. While the belief in the second coming of Jesus remained a part of Christian doctrine generally, those who prepared themselves for his imminent return were a minority who proclaimed their message to the masses only in times of acute crisis. Strictly speaking, Judaism did not really have a uniform teaching about the Messiah. Nevertheless, the figure of the Messiah belonged both to popular religion as well as to scribal theory. We can read a good deal of Jewish literature without finding any references to the Messiah. In the Mishna, for example, the Messiah is mentioned just twice! On the other hand, the Messiah is mentioned frequently in synagogue prayers and in the scribal exegesis of Scripture. There were scarcely any scribes who openly questioned the expectation of the Messiah. The silence in parts of the literature, including many apocalypses, is surprising, but that silence is hard to interpret. The question which can be raised, though scarcely answered, is suggested by the motto of the Zealots, "We have no other king than God." Did this involve not only the renunciation of the rights of all foreign rulers but also the idea of a direct theocracy (which had a biblical basis in 1 Samuel 8 and 10), which did not regard the restoration of the Israelite kingdom as a legitimate political or religious goal?

What is perhaps most surprising when we turn from the New Testament to Jewish literature is the fact that even the technical term *Messiah* ("the anointed one") is hardly attested prior to the time of Jesus. The term *Messiah* is not used alone, but with qualifying words and phrases such as "God's Messiah" ("the anointed of the Lord"), "the Messiah of Israel," and so on. Most likely the term *Messiah*, as we find it in the New Testament, originated as an abbreviation of the phrase "God's Messiah." Strictly speaking, such an expression was not without ambiguity, because it was possible to claim that not only kings but also priests and prophets were anointed by God. But we can confidently claim that the idea of the king as God's anointed was the primary meaning which would immediately be assumed, unless otherwise indicated by the context. That would be true even though anointing was a ritual associated with the installation of high priests. The occasional application of the expression "anointed one" to prophets is obviously secondary and presupposes a metaphorical use of the term "anoint" in connection with the communication of the Holy Spirit (cf. Isa. 61:1). One of the more interesting aspects of the application of the phrase "the Lord's anointed" to prophets lies in the fact that it says something essential about how anointing was understood. If the catechetical answer to the question, "Why is the king called the Lord's anointed?" was, "Because he was anointed with God's spirit," then further perspectives and new possible combinations are open. That becomes clear if we formulate the obvious conclusion in this way: "the one who is anointed with the Spirit of God is the Messiah."

It is abundantly clear in the New Testament that the term *Messiah* is simply the title of the future king, the savior king. One could even regard it as his "name." Wherever the term *Messiah* (or *Christ*) is defined it is clear that it is a royal title. That implies that the term is not primarily associated with the symbol of anointing but with royal status. This certainly reflects the normal Jewish conception, also when the fuller expression "God's anointed" was retained. Yet it was always possible to reflect upon the literal meaning of the expression. This meaning must have been conscious at Qumran, where the Messiah of Israel was named alongside of the Messiah of Aaron. These phrases refer to the eschatological king and his high priest. They are coordinated by virtue of the fact that they are both anointed by God. Here it is also worth noting that it is in a context which mentions both that *Messiah* is used as a royal title, while otherwise the characteristic title in these texts is usually *prince of the congregation* (a designation inspired by Ezek. 34:24 and chapters 40–48).

Originally, the conception of a Messiah derived its content from the Israelite royal ideology. But our primary interest is in what was generally associated with the title at the time of Jesus. The answer is not so simple, because it depends on entire eschatological scenarios, and they exhibit great diversity. At this point it is appropriate that we become more specific by reproducing the classic description of the Messiah from Psalms of Solomon 17. We must hasten to point out that here we are dealing with traditional Jewish future expectation which has a decidedly this-worldly focus and lacks all typically apocalyptic features. In Pss. Sol. 17:21-46 we read (trans. R. B. Wright, in *OTP*, 2:667-669):

> See, Lord, and raise up for them their king,
> > the son of David, to rule over your servant Israel
> > in the time known to you, O God.
> Undergird him with the strength to destroy the unrighteous rulers,
> > to purge Jerusalem from gentiles
> > who trample her to destruction;
> > in wisdom and in righteousness to drive out
> > the sinners from the inheritance;
> to smash the arrogance of sinners
> > like a potter's jar;
> To shatter all their substance with an iron rod;
> to destroy the unlawful nations with the word of his mouth;
> At his warning the nations will flee from his presence;
> > and he will condemn sinners by the thoughts of their hearts.
> He will gather a holy people
> > whom he will lead in righteousness;
> and he will judge the tribes of the people
> > that have been made holy by the Lord their God.
> He will not tolerate unrighteousness (even) to pause among them,
> > and any person who knows wickedness shall not live with them.
> For he shall know them
> > that they are all children of their God.

He will distribute them upon the land
    according to their tribes;
the alien and the foreigner will no longer live near them.
He will judge peoples and nations in the wisdom
      of his righteousness. . . .
And he will have gentile nations serving him under his yoke,
    and he will glorify the Lord in (a place) prominent (above)
      the whole earth.
And he will purge Jerusalem
    (and make it) holy as it was even from the beginning.
(for) nations to come from the ends of the earth to see his glory,
    to bring as gifts her children who had been driven out,
and to see the glory of the Lord
    with which God has glorified her.
And he will be a righteous king over them, taught by God.
There will be no unrighteousness among them in his days,
    for all shall be holy,
    and their king shall be the Lord Messiah.
(For) he will not rely on horse and rider and bow,
    nor will he collect gold and silver for war.
Nor will he build up hope in a multitude for a day of war.
The Lord himself is his king,
    and the hope of the one who has a strong hope in God.
He shall be compassionate to all the nations
    (who) reverently (stand) before him.
He will strike the earth with the word of his mouth forever;
    he will bless the Lord's people with wisdom and happiness.
And he himself (will be) free from sin, (in order) to rule a
      great people.
He will expose officials and drive out sinners
    by the strength of his word.
And he will not weaken in his days, (relying) on his God,
    for God made him
    powerful in the holy spirit
    and wise in the counsel of understanding,
    with strength and righteousness.
And the blessing of the Lord will be with him in strength,
    and he will not weaken;
His hope (will be) in the Lord.
Then who will succeed against him,

mighty in his actions
and strong in the fear of God?
Faithfully and righteously shepherding the Lord's flock,
he will not let any of them stumble in their pasture.
He will lead them all in holiness
· and there will be no arrogance among them,
that any should be oppressed.
This is the beauty of the king of Israel
which God knew,
to raise him over the house of Israel
to discipline it.
His words will be purer than the finest gold, the best.
He will judge the peoples in the assemblies,
the tribes of the sanctified.
His words will be as the words of the holy ones,
among sanctified peoples.
Blessed are those born in those days
to see the good fortune of Israel
which God will bring to pass in the assembly of the tribes.
May God dispatch his mercy to Israel;
may he deliver us from the pollution of profane enemies;
The Lord himself is our king forevermore.

We could also have included a selection from Psalms of Solomon 18, but that would not add anything new. The translation is partly uncertain since the Greek text behind it is a very unclear and mechanical translation of a lost Hebrew original which is dated to the middle of the first century B.C. and ascribed to a Pharisaic author.

The text is a prayer that God will soon restore the kingdom to Israel, drive out her heathen oppressors, and reunite the dispersed tribes, giving them their heritage in the holy land and granting them a glorious and blessed future upon the earth. Most remarkable is the extraordinary degree to which the theme of the restoration of the kingdom predominates. The son of David, the Lord's anointed, is the central symbol. Salvation comes both with and through him. He is depicted as the perfect ruler in agreement with the classical Israelite ideal of kingship but with a pronounced softening of the militaristic element, just as in the well-known messianic prophecies in Isaiah 9 and 11 (and many others, cf. Micah 4 and 5:1-3; Amos 9:11-13; Jer. 23:5-6; 30:8-9,18-22; 33:14-25; Zech. 9:9-10; Ezek.

34:23-31; 37:22-28). In all probability all these texts originated in the postexilic period, yet the kingship ideal is found in Psalms from the period of the monarchy, e.g., Ps. 7:2. The great emphasis placed on the king's piety and uprightness should be underscored. This manifests itself in moral blamelessness and incorruptible righteousness, and his banishing everything that is wrong and immoral in the land. He also renounces all military, political, and economic security and places all his confidence in God's power and righteousness, because it is really God himself who is the legitimate king of Israel. The Messiah is actually a theocratic symbol. It is somewhat surprising that the king is depicted as an individual rather than the founder of a new dynasty, since he is not expected to live forever. Yet that is a common feature of messianic prophecies. In the apocalyptic adaptation of this motif, the time of salvation is made to coincide with the lifetime of the savior king (which can, however, be stretched out to 1000 years). In the Psalms of Solomon, as in the classical messianic prophesies, the obvious explanation is simply that the entire focus of attention is upon the restoration of the kingdom and the installation of the new king. There is nothing in the Psalms of Solomon which suggests a supernatural Messiah. He is in all respects simply what people expected the ideal king to be. The utopian exaggerations are really part and parcel of the image of the ideal king. In relation to a poetic prophecy like Isa. 11:1-10, which describes paradisiacal conditions, the description in the Psalms of Solomon is relatively restrained.

The antimilitaristic traits in the conception of the Messiah as a Prince of Peace require emphasis. The Psalms of Solomon can be understood as a reaction to the militaristic kingdom experienced under the Hasmoneans, yet the theme itself is much older. Even though the dream of peace is widespread and probably universal, many of the descriptions of the Messiah trace the distinctive idea of a king who is different from other kings and correspondingly of a kingdom which is, so to speak, not of this world, because violence and injustice do not exist and there is not even the thought of war. In the familiar depiction of the kingdom of peace in Mic. 4:1-4 (cf. Isa. 2:2-4), the temple of the Lord is a symbol of salvation. The king is not mentioned, for the theocracy is apparently direct. Yet it may well be that the figure of the king was tacitly understood and not suppressed (cf. v. 3, where the subject would normally be the

Messiah, and the clear messianic prophecy in 5:1-4). Micah 4:1-4 reads:

It shall come to pass in the latter days
    that the mountain of the house of the Lord
shall be established as the highest of the mountains,
    and shall be raised up above the hills;
and peoples shall flow to it,
    and many nations shall come, and say:
"Come, let us go up to the mountain of the Lord,
    to the house of the God of Jacob;
that he may teach us his ways
    and we may walk in his paths."
For out of Zion shall go forth the law,
    and the word of the Lord from Jerusalem.
He shall judge between many peoples,
    and shall decide for strong nations afar off;
and they shall beat their swords into plowshares,
    and their spears into pruning hooks;
nation shall not lift up sword against nation,
    neither shall they learn war any more;
but they shall sit every man under his vine and under his fig tree,
    and none shall make them afraid;
    for the mouth of the Lord of hosts has spoken.

Here Israel's temple is the navel of the earth, the center which attracts everyone, and the place from which the law of God is disseminated, yet scarcely any political nationalism remains. Several messianic prophecies are almost equally peaceful and idyllic, as Jer. 23:5-6,

Behold, the days are coming, says the Lord,
    when I will raise up for David a righteous Branch,
and he shall reign as king and deal wisely,
    and shall execute justice and righteousness in the land.
In his days Judah will be saved,
    and Israel will dwell securely.
And this is the name which he will be called:
    "The Lord is our righteousness."

The God-given king is the guarantee of peace and righteousness. In Isa. 9:2-7 he is given the names "Wonderful Counselor, Mighty God, Everlasting Father, Prince of Peace" (v. 6). In Isaiah 11 it is said, among other things, "the Spirit of the Lord shall rest upon him, the spirit of wisdom and understanding, the spirit of counsel and might, the spirit of knowledge and the fear of the Lord." Zechariah 9:9-10 speaks of a humble king who makes his entry on an ass, a picture which seems almost a parody of the royal majesty. He eradicates all weapons and creates peace on the earth.

The Messiah is not portrayed as a mighty oriental king. He is not an Israelite counterpart to Cyrus or Alexander (some of the texts may well come from the Hellenistic period), but rather a religious hero who obviously does not derive his authority on the strength of personal military triumphs, but rather receives it as a miraculous gift and a holy task assigned by almighty God. The fact that the Messiah functions as a theocratic symbol must again be emphasized. His king is God, and it is God who is the everlasting king of Israel, just as we find in Psalms of Solomon 17. Otherwise we must certainly observe that this psalm, even though it strongly emphasizes the piety and holiness of the king, has a decisively temporal orientation and places a strong emphasis on nationalistic themes. That is quite understandable, since it was written after the dissolution of the Hasmonean kingdom when the Romans were masters in the holy land. Political experiences are reflected both in the image of the Messiah and in the dream of a time of salvation.

Political experiences are also reflected in the texts to which we now turn, the Testaments of the Twelve Patriarchs and the literature from Qumran. It is natural to place these groups of texts together, despite the facts that copies of the Testaments were not found at Qumran and that they have little in common with Essene sectarianism. However, in both collections of texts we find similar ideas about two coordinated persons or offices to which the hope of deliverance is tied, the anointed king and, more prominently, the anointed priest. The basis and primary scriptural foundation for this conception is Zechariah 4, which was originally a specific prophecy about the Davidic descendant Zerubbabel and the high priest Joshua. The prophet Zechariah tied Israel's hopes for restoration to both of these individuals. Later, a basis was found in the Law itself, namely, in Balaam's prophecy about the star (= the priest) and the scepter

(= the king) in Num. 24:17. The developing historical situation again makes it understandable that the high priest stands in the foreground. During the long period when there was no Israelite king, the high priest gradually became the spiritual leader, unifying symbol, and primary spokesman for Jewish affairs. But in the same way in which the dream of an ideal king of the end time reflected the loss of an actual contemporary king, the development of the expectation of a perfect priest of the end time was connected to a current crisis in the office of the high priest. This is very clear with regard to the Qumran community, who considered the Hasmonean high priests as illegitimate, false priests who had usurped the position which rightly belonged to the legitimate Zadokite priests of Qumran. In the Testaments of the Twelve Patriarchs it is very difficult to untangle the historical background, because they have been subject to "updating," making it impossible to reconstruct the various phases of textual history. When even Test. Judah 24 speaks not only of the coming king from Judah (symbolized by the scepter in Num. 24:17), but first mentions the priest (= the star from Jacob), one can only wonder whether the original prediction has been suppressed in favor of the priest. The Greek translation in this case exhibits a thorough Christian revision, but the much shorter Armenian translation may well preserve a more purely Jewish form (even though the Armenian version has also undergone Christian revision). Here is Test. Judah 24 (trans. H. C. Kee, in *OTP*, 1:801):

> And after this there shall arise for you a Star from Jacob in peace.
> . . . And the heavens will be opened upon him to pour out the spirit
> as a blessing of the Holy Father. And he will pour the spirit of grace
> on you. And you shall be sons in truth, and you will walk in his first
> and final decrees. . . . Then he will illumine the scepter of my kingdom, and from your root will arise the Shoot, and through it will arise
> the rod of righteousness for the nations, to judge and to save all that
> call on the Lord.

In some respects it is easier to understand this text as Christian rather than as Jewish, so no presumptions can be made about details. But the interpretation of Num. 24:17 itself as a prophecy of the eschatological priest and the eschatological king is Jewish, since it also appears in the Essene texts (Damascus Document 7:18-20; War Scroll 11:6). There is also a reference to Num. 24:17 in Test. Levi

18:3, though only to the star—since the entire chapter is devoted to the eschatological priest who completely assimilates typically messianic features. In this case it is hopeless to attempt to reconstruct the pre-Christian wording. Certainly, many scholars have attempted to construe the text as Jewish, but this is methodologically risky when it is known that the Testaments of the Twelve Patriarchs as a whole has been edited by Christians and that many formulations can more easily be understood as Christian applications of prophecies to Jesus than as originally Jewish themes. Test. Levi 18 was undoubtedly an originally Jewish text, but it has been revised and, as it now stands, it must be regarded as a vehicle for ecclesiastical Christology. The Jewish text probably said something about the king from Judah (= the scepter), but that cannot be demonstrated. Since the Jewish original cannot be reconstructed we are compelled to leave this interesting text out of consideration.

There are similar problems with all the prophetic sections of the Test. 12 Patr. to the extent that the only elements which can be utilized as certain evidence for Jewish conceptions are themes which are more easily construed as Jewish than as Christian. In some cases the secondary Christian reinterpretation seems to be fairly clearly defined because it appears in short and conspicuous additions to the text. Test. Simeon 7:1-2 (trans. H. C. Kee, in *OTP*, 1:787), provides an example when we bracket the words which are obviously Christian interpolations:

> And now, my children, be obedient to Levi and to Judah. Do not exalt yourselves above these two tribes, [because from them will arise the Savior come from God]. For the Lord will raise up from Levi someone as high priest and from Judah someone as king [God and man]. He will save all the gentiles and the tribe of Israel.

That the phrase "God and man" is a Christian gloss requires no argument. The second phrase gives itself away not simply by mentioning that salvation includes *all* people (a possible sentiment in Jewish wisdom literature), but by the fact that the Gentiles are mentioned before Israel.

Many scholars attempt to proceed by simply placing brackets around such obvious glosses, thereby indicating that what remains is a Jewish text. But this procedure cannot be carried out to any convincing extent. The problem is that the Christian revision of the

Test. 12 Patr. probably took place in several stages. It could, for example, have been the last Christian copyist who is responsible for the most obvious glosses, while earlier copyists could well have reworked the text in quite different ways, such as by inserting longer additions.

Among the many typical Jewish insertions concerning Levi and Judah found in the Test. 12 Patr. is the following from Test. Judah 21:1-4 (trans. Kee, in *OTP*, 1:800), where Judah is presented as the speaker:

> And now, children, love Levi so that you may endure. Do not be arrogant toward him or you will be wholly destroyed. To me God has given the kingship and to him the priesthood; and he has subjected the kingship to the priesthood. To me he gave earthly matters and to Levi, heavenly matters. As heaven is superior to the earth, so is God's priesthood superior to the kingdom on earth, unless through sin it falls away from the Lord and is dominated by the earthly kingdom.

An Aramaic fragment from Qumran is obviously related: "the kingship is for you and your sons. The priesthood is superior to the kingship." Though perhaps not expressed quite so clearly, it is evident from various statements in the Qumran texts that there was a marked tendency in Qumran to give the messianic priest precedence over the messianic king. To that extent it can be claimed that it is the Essene view that finds expression in the sections on Levi and Judah in the Test. 12 Patr. Since we need not deal with the problem of Christian interpolations in the texts from Qumran, we turn to them further to illuminate the expectation of the two anointed ones of the last days.

In the Manual of Discipline (1QS), an admonition is found in column 9 of the expanded version to the effect that all must follow exactly the original regulations of the community "until the prophet and the anointed ones of Aaron and Israel come" (1QS 9.11). This is the only place where the prophet is mentioned. In the Damascus Document (CD 12.23; 14.19; 19.1f.; 20.1), we find very similar statements, though with the major difference that the ambiguous form "the anointed of Aaron and Israel" is used. Many scholars have maintained that this indicates a single individual, the Messiah. But in all probability we are dealing with *two* persons, a Messiah from Aaron, the anointed high priest of the end time, and the Messiah from Israel, the king of the restored kingdom. Both figures occur in other connections.

Particularly important (and also relevant for the problem of the use of messianic designations), is the addition to the Manual of Discipline (designated 1QSa), the Rule of the Congregation. This text contains an idealistic description of the situation at the end time with instructions for all the people, and particularly for the sacral meal to be celebrated when the Messiah comes. Unfortunately, the text is uncertain at the most crucial point. According to the generally accepted reading, the eschatological king is introduced simply as "the Messiah," while the eschatological high priest is simply designated "the priest" (1QSa 2.12). Further on, the title "the Messiah of Israel" is used (1QSa 2.14, 20). Here it is prescribed that all the priests seat themselves in their own places before the king and his officers. The priest, after he has blessed the meal, is also the first to partake. It is perhaps not so surprising if the priest has precedence in a cultic setting at a sacral meal, yet it also agrees with the fact that Aaron is customarily mentioned before Israel. Most astonishing, however, is the fact that the War Scroll barely mentions the prince, while the priests play a completely dominant role in the idealized description of the 40-year war between the sons of light and the sons of darkness. One could certainly assume that the war would be the affair of the king, though it is described in a strikingly unrealistic manner. It is, however, not always easy to decide who is referred to. One may, for example, wonder whether, in 1QM 11:6, where Num. 24:17 is cited, it is not actually the Messiah who is referred to. Here mention of either the king or the priest would be appropriate. In the so-called Testimonia (4QTestim), there is a collection of biblical texts which mention the prophet who will come (Deut. 18:18f.), the king (Num. 24:15-17), and the priest (Num. 24:15-17; Deut. 33:8-11). In the Damascus Document (CD 7.18-20) it is expressly stated that "the star" is "the interpreter of the Law," a term which characterizes the primary task of the high priest, while "the scepter" is "the prince of all the people," which is the title for the future king which occurs most often in the Qumran texts.

The text which reveals the most about what the king stands for is Blessings (1QSb, or Appendix B to 1QS), an extremely fragmentary text which seems originally to have contained very lengthy formulas of blessing for use in the messianic period. Three introductory formulas are preserved, suggesting that what follows relates to the whole community (the people), the priests, and the king, respectively. Since large portions are missing, it is possible that there were several sections. For inadequate reasons, Joseph Milik, the editor of the fragments, presupposes that the blessing for the people was followed by a blessing for the high priest. In my view, that is based on a misunderstanding.[1] It is also difficult to imagine a special blessing for the high priest, because it is more natural that he is the one who pronounces the blessing. That is confirmed by the fact that the blessing for the people consists of a long paraphrase of the Aaronic blessing of Num. 6:24-26. But with the blessing for the priesthood there are, to be sure, some indications which clearly refer to the glory of the high priest ("a diadem for the most holy one"), and which especially emphasize how he becomes a light for the whole world because of his knowledge and insight. Only the first part of the blessing for the king is preserved (1QSb 5:20-29). It basically consists of a paraphrase of some famous messianic passages (Isa. 11:1-5; Gen. 49:9; Mic. 4:13; Num. 24:17), and sketches a very traditional picture of the ideal king along the lines of that found in Psalms of Solomon 17. He will renew the covenant and establish an eternal kingdom, judge the lowly with justice, and walk blamelessly in the path of God. Filled with wisdom and a God-fearing spirit, he will eliminate the ungodly. Militaristic features also stand out prominently. He will rule over the earth and trample on the people as one tramples upon rubbish lying on the road. All nations will serve him.

It is noteworthy that here, in a text so strongly reflecting the community's own ideology, there is such a traditional and nationalistic messianic ideal. That can be explained by the fact that the community adapted a well-worked-out exegetical tradition together with an arsenal of supporting messianic texts. In addition to those already mentioned, we should notice that Nathan's speech to David in 2 Sam. 7:11-14 is a messianic text of central importance. This means that a king was expected from the house of David. David's fallen booth will be restored (Amos 9:11; cf. 4QFlor). Here lies the primary reason for calling the Messiah the son of God. The fact should also be mentioned that the Temple Scroll, which, among the Dead Sea Scrolls, contains the most extensive idealized regulations for the eschatological temple state following the pattern of Ezekiel 40–47, also includes laws concerning the king (56.12-59.21; cf.

Deut. 17:14-20). Even though these laws are greatly expanded in scope, in principle they contribute nothing really new. It is worth noticing that the king must practice strict monogamy—even divorce is out of the question—and he must marry one of the daughters of the land. Even if the king is the commander-in-chief and is always surrounded by 12,000 noble and God-fearing fighting men, his military contribution appears limited to wars of defense. It is strongly enjoined that he must not begin a campaign without first submitting the matter to the priest for approval, who, with the aid of the Urim and Thummim (Exod. 28:30), decides what is the will of God. It is also remarkable how dependent the king is on his council, which consists of 12 rulers, 12 priests, and 12 Levites. They will instruct him in the Law, and he must not do anything without the consent of the council. A king who acts in accordance with his own desires will be removed from office, a measure applying both to himself and to his descendants. There is, accordingly, no mention of an individual Messiah. The good king, and his sons after him, will reign long in the land. The Temple Scroll describes an everlasting ideal state and is unconcerned with messianic figures. Actually, the term "everlasting" is not quite correct, for even the fantastic temple complex which is described will finally be replaced by one not made with hands, but by God.

The priests at Qumran held fast to the hope of the restoration of the Davidic kingdom, and did not replace the notion of that kingdom with a more direct form of theocracy. Yet they made the king completely subject to the priests because they were the connecting link between God and people. It is they who had the authority to interpret the Law and were able to transmit orders to the king regarding the will of God. For the Qumran community it was undoubtedly more important to reinstate the legitimate priesthood and reestablish the proper cultic worship in Jerusalem than to restore the kingdom of David. Yet while the anointed priest is placed by the side of the anointed king, it appears clear that "the anointed one," the Messiah, is still king. In later texts in the Mishna (ca. A.D. 200), the anointing of the high priest plays an important role, and there the term "the anointed one" can be used precisely of him. Here the ointment itself has become an eschatological symbol. It disappeared with the high priest Joshua (cf. Zech. 3:4f.; 4:14; 6:11-13), but will be rediscovered in the last days. The Qumran texts provide no examples of any corresponding conceptions. The Temple Scroll, in fact, has surprisingly little to say about the high priest.

The eschatological conceptions of the Temple Scroll are vague and internally inconsistent. Utopian and fantastic ideas about the holy city and the temple are combined with a law concerning the king which, while certainly not realistic, nevertheless reckons with royal succession and the possibility of impeaching kings who go their own way. Other texts instead give the impression that the Messiah is an individual king of the end time who is a perfect, ideal figure. The anointed priest, on the other hand, has no individual characteristics. He is simply the high priest of the messianic age, the interpreter of the Law, who stands beside the Messiah. If to some extent we get another impression from the Testaments of the Twelve Patriarchs, particularly from Test. Levi 18, where we apparently have a priestly Messiah who makes the king fairly redundant, this is the result of the tendentious rewriting of the text both by Jewish and Christian redactors on various occasions. This document can hardly be used to prove that there were social settings where the priestly messiah was a real competitor to the royal Messiah. Even in Essene circles it can hardly be claimed that the eschatological priest appears as an eschatological savior figure. Rather, he is the indispensable counselor whom the savior king has by his side, and, as such, he is a symbol of the kingdom's dependence on God's mercy.

In popular expectation, the high priest of the end time played no role as long as the temple and the sacrificial cultus were functioning in Jerusalem. This makes good sense, since it was only the Essenes of Qumran who, because the cult was headed by an illegitimate priest, wanted to have nothing to do with the temple. They were therefore restricted to fantasizing about a future ideal state of affairs.

For a short period under the Hasmoneans, Israel had the experience of being a relatively independent state under the leadership of priest-kings. One might suppose that this would stimulate the formation of a new messianic ideal with king and priest in one person. Yet there is very little in the literature which points in this direction. The circles of the religious trend-setters did not accept the Hasmonean union of royal and priestly offices in one person. God had given the kingdom to the tribe of Judah and the house of David, while the priesthood was reserved for the tribe of Levi and the descendants of Aaron. The peculiar combination of the two offices in the person of Jesus in the letter to the Hebrews (with the aid of biblical statements about Melchizedek in Genesis 14 and Ps. 110:4) has no demonstrable basis in Jewish thought.[2]

It is probable that there were those in the court of the Hasmonean princes who wanted both to defend and extol the combination of spiritual and temporal authority in one person. Yet even 1 Maccabees rather gives the impression that the arrangement was defended as a historically conditioned interim solution, and not promoted as a lasting religious ideal. According to 1 Macc. 14:41 a decision was made to make the military leader Simon into the leader of the people and the high priest "for ever"—"until a trustworthy prophet should arise." It seems as if the decision contained a diplomatically worded reservation in order to be acceptable to those who looked forward to an eschatological fulfillment of the messianic promises. When even the Essenes at Qumran held fast to the expectation of a royal Messiah, a partial explanation can be found in the fact that they distanced themselves in principle from the Hasmonean union of temporal and spiritual authority. The Essenes attended to their primary concern, the restoration of the legitimate priesthood, by allowing the anointed king to have an anointed priest at his side, and by emphasizing the king's dependence on the priestly role of mediating and interpreting the Law and will of God.

The priestly Messiah can certainly not be considered an alternative to the royal Messiah. During Jesus' time the term *Messiah* signified only the eschatological savior-king. It was he who was the symbol of salvation. There is not the slightest trace in the New Testament of a Jewish expectation of an eschatological high priest, unless the attempt is made to sneak the theme in by attempting to demonstrate that the end-time Elijah should be regarded as a priest as well as a prophet. One should hesitate to do that, for even though John the Baptist (who was identified with Elijah) belonged to a priestly family, according to Luke, there is nothing which indicates that John/Elijah is depicted in a priestly role. Moreover, there is scarcely any reliable pre-Christian Jewish evidence for identifying Elijah with the eschatological high priest.

The final prophet

While the eschatological priest could not replace the figure of the king in future expectation, the idea of an end-time prophet was much more independent. He could very well appear as the only

human actor. On the other hand, he could also easily be dispensed
with or else combined with other figures. The idea of a final prophet
is ultimately based on Deut. 18:15,18, where God promises to raise
up a new prophet like Moses. The original meaning of this text is
that, when Moses dies, another will take over. God will make pro-
vision that there will always be a prophet to lead Israel. Later the
statement was interpreted in quite different ways: as specific instructions that Joshua should be Moses' successor, or as a prediction
of famous prophets of history, or as an eschatological promise that
God, in the last days, would have mercy on his people by sending
them a new Moses who would finally liberate the elect people and
bestow eternal blessedness upon them. Against the background of
the deplorable Jewish historical experience since the fall of Jerusalem
and the Babylonian captivity, it was only natural that scribes found
hope and consolation in an eschatological understanding of Deuteronomy 18. For the Samaritans, who recognized only the five books
of Moses as canonical, this prophecy became a primary "messianic"
confession. It was given a fixed liturgical setting following the Deca-
log of Exodus 20. The Samaritans, who had broken with Jerusalem
and united around their own sanctuary on Gerizim, could not very
well link their future hope to a new David on Zion. They hoped
rather for a new prophet like Moses. It is conceivable that Jewish
animosity toward everything Samaritan explains why the eschatological exploitation of Deuteronomy 18 plays such a strikingly insignificant role in Jewish texts. An eschatological interpretation is
found at Qumran, but in a form which does not turn the Prophet
into a savior figure, but regards him as the least prominent member
of a triumvirate. When he is mentioned before the anointed ones of
Aaron and Israel (lQS 9.11; cf. 4QTestim), that does not at all
suggest his precedence, but rather alludes to the fact that he is a
kind of forerunner, the one who appears first chronologically and
foreshadows the messianic era. It also means that in the last days
the three classical charismatic "offices" of prophet, king, and priest
will be restored. Nevertheless, the motif of this eschatological triumvirate is not prominent in the texts. This probably has a perfectly
natural explanation in the fact that there was no real necessity for
a special prophet (i.e., no real place for him), because the prophetic
functions could be exercised equally well by other charismatic figures who were also anointed by the Spirit. At Qumran there was no

need for a special prophet beside the anointed priest who was the right teacher and interpreter of the Law. The organization and ideology of the Qumran community, with its strict leadership hierarchy and distinctive orientation to Scripture, meant that there really was no place for free prophets with direct revelations. A long process of development had taken place with respect to Israelite prophets. When or how temple prophets disappeared as an institution is not known. It must have occurred in conjunction with the partial assumption of their functions by priests and Levites. Other prophetic functions were probably unsuitable for the normal pattern of religious life. When Holy Scripture was elevated to the highest authority, scribes took over the role of interpreting God's revelation. Yet the idea of prophetic revelation was a firmly fixed notion, and people lamented the fact that the time of the prophets was past. Yet at the same time they made it more and more impossible for a real prophet with a new revelation to appear with the requisite religious authority. One aspect of the prophetic spirit certainly lived on in the form of the inspired exegesis of Scripture as found in apocalyptic literature. Yet this literature was characteristically either anonymous or pseudonymous and did not easily win acceptance. In a society dominated by an organized priesthood and regulated by religious laws and traditions, prophetic phenomena and pretensions were inevitably greeted with skepticism. Nevertheless, prophecy was part of tradition and was a permanent feature of dreams of a golden age. The restoration of prophecy through God once more sending his Holy Spirit fit in quite naturally with expectations of salvation. But that did not need to occur in the precise form of the idea of the eschatological prophet. The prophet Joel says that in the last days God will pour out his Spirit upon all people so that even slaves will speak prophetically (cf. Acts 2:17f.).[3]

Actually, the expectation of the end-time prophet may have had little to do with the hope of the restoration of the spirit of prophecy. Of course, Moses was regarded as the greatest of all prophets, but even so he is not an obvious model for the prophetic role. The formula "Moses *and* the prophets" was commonly used and, even though the Law and Prophets were meant (the latter term also included the historical books from Joshua to 2 Kings), that also suggests that Moses was placed in a unique category. The belief that God would one day send a prophet like Moses was not primarily associated with the notion that classical prophecy would be reborn, but that people would receive a new leader and savior who would deliver Israel with extraordinary power. In other words, people imagined a prophetic, miracle-working Messiah. In that respect there was little difference between a new Moses and a new David. While the Samaritans were united in the dream of a Moses *redivivus*, the Jews held fast to the traditional conception of the Messiah, the son of David. Yet, the latter conception could certainly be colored by features from Moses in keeping with the whole Exodus typology, i.e., the tendency to imagine the final deliverance by analogy to the liberation from Egypt and the entry into the promised land. Josephus mentions several individuals who, in the period before A.D. 70, appeared as would-be messianic prophets who convinced people to believe that God would accomplish wonders similar to those he had performed in the days of Moses and Joshua. Although the idea of Moses *redivivus* seems to have played an insignificant role for the Jews of Jesus' time, conceptions of the Messiah borrowed many features from typology of the Exodus and of Moses. There are faint indications that the figures of Moses and the Messiah were combined, but the evidence is vague and problematical. Considering the place of Moses in Jewish consciousness, it would have been unthinkable to demote the new or risen Moses to the status of a mere forerunner of the Messiah.

It was in another form and using a different scriptural foundation that the notion of an end-time prophet became a particularly popular theme in Jewish eschatology. This was the expectation that Elijah, who had been taken alive into heaven, would come again to prepare Israel for God's own coming in judgment. A biblical basis was found in the concluding statements of the last prophetic book, Malachi. In Mal. 3:1 we read, "Behold, I send my messenger [Hebrew: *mal'aki*] to prepare the way before me." This is expanded in an appendix in Mal. 4:5f.: "Behold, I will send you Elijah the prophet before the great and terrible day of the Lord comes. And he will turn the hearts of the fathers to their children, and the hearts of children to their fathers, lest I come and smite the land with a curse." The Septuagint has: "he will turn the heart of the father back to the son, and the heart of a man to his neighbor." This passage is referred to in Sir. 48:10, which, after an enumeration of Elijah's historical achievements, continues: "You who are ready at the appointed time, [as] it is written, to calm the wrath of God before it breaks out in fury, to turn the heart of the father to the son, and to restore the tribes of Jacob." Here Elijah is given a twofold task. First, he will motivate the people to repent so that judgment may be avoided when God begins his righteous judgment. Second, he will restore the 12 ancient tribes, and so gather all people of Israelite descent, all of Abraham's children, to the holy land. In Psalms of Solomon 17 and in other texts, this final task is associated with the Messiah.

In the popular view, Elijah was no less important than the Messiah (even today a cup is prepared for Elijah at Jewish passover meals!). Elijah is the one whom God sends ahead to put all things in order (cf. Mark 9:11; Matt. 17:14). In Malachi it is the coming of God himself for which Elijah prepares. The Messiah is not mentioned. But it was certainly not very difficult to combine the idea of a final prophet who would preach repentance before the judgment with the expectation of the Messiah and the restoration of the kingdom of David by transforming Elijah into a forerunner of the Messiah, as the New Testament assumes. Justin Martyr (died ca. A.D. 156) mentions the Jewish view that Elijah must point out the Messiah and anoint him.[4] This corresponds to one feature in the enumeration of Elijah's achievements in Sirach 48, that the prophet anointed kings to serve as agents of God's vengeance.

While it makes good sense that the promise of a prophet like Moses in Deuteronomy 18 could have been combined with the prophecy of Elijah in Malachi 4 so that Elijah would be identified with "the Prophet," it cannot be demonstrated that this actually happened. In the New Testament Moses and Elijah are carefully kept distinct from each other (e.g., John 1:21f.). Yet there are indications that the Prophet could be identified with the Messiah (e.g. John 6:14f.). In the Qumran literature there are no indications that the Prophet was thought to be Elijah. A few scholars have nonetheless contended that the eschatological high priest was identified with Elijah, but there is very little evidence to confirm that view either. (The theory that Elijah belonged to the tribe of Levi rather than Gad or Benjamin, as certain traditions maintain, is found among rabbinic sages, based on the fact that Elijah offered a sacrifice on Mount Carmel, 1 Kings 20).

The returning Elijah is the eschatological figure who actually competes with the Messiah in popular imagination, perhaps even in scribal speculation. At the same time, he is the figure most easily connected with the Messiah. When they are linked, it is always the Messiah who is the more prominent figure and who symbolizes the consummation, while Elijah is the forerunner and herald who nearly completes his role when he, as a prophet, has designated and anointed God's Messiah.

The Servant of the Lord and the suffering righteous one

We have just described the eschatological figures who played significant roles in Jewish eschatology. It is reasonable to ask whether Jesus identified himself with any of them. But we must first discuss the figure of the Servant in the remarkable series of songs found in Deutero-Isaiah, even though the "Servant" does not occur as the designation of any particular figure in Jewish hopes for the future. Even in the four songs themselves (Isa. 42:1-4; 49:1-6; 50:4-11; 52:13—53:12), it is not clear whether the figure of the Servant is a single individual, and therefore it is uncertain whether there is sufficient reason for capitalizing the term *Servant* and conceptualizing him or her as one person or one concept. Scholars are not agreed about who the poet himself was referring to and what he meant, particularly in the case of the last and most important of the songs. This, however, is a complex issue which we cannot discuss. We can only state with some confidence that Deutero-Isaiah was *not* referring to a future eschatological figure. The most interesting point for us is whether the Servant has, in one way or other, become incorporated into eschatological expectations in such a way that the basic ideals and conceptions of other eschatological figures have been affected. The view has long been popular among New Testament scholars that Jesus identified himself as the Messiah because he read these songs as prophecies of the Messiah. For him the Messiah was primarily the Suffering Servant of the Lord. Some scholars have maintained that this was a new and original understanding of these prophetic texts. Others claim to have found this view reflected in Jewish documents written before the time of Jesus. However, some scholars are now of the opinion that it was in fact the Christian community which, against the background of Jesus' suffering and death, understood Isaiah 53 as a prophecy of the Messiah who would suffer and die as an atonement for the sins of people.

One firm point of departure is the fact that there are many texts in the New Testament which cite the Servant Songs or allude to them (Matt. 8:17; 12:18-21; Acts 1:8; 8:32f.; 13:47; Luke 22:37; John 12:38; Rom. 10:16; 15:21; 1 Pet. 2:24f.; and probably others also, particularly Mark 10:45). In Acts, moreover, the designation *servant* (Greek: *pais*) is connected to Jesus. But it is unclear whether this should encourage us to think of the Servant of Deutero-Isaiah, for the phrase "the servant of God" is also a religious title of honor and it is precisely with that connotation that it is used of Jesus (Acts 3:13,26; 4:27, 30; cf. Matt. 12:18). It is used of David as well (Acts 4:25; cf. Luke 1:69). There is no doubt that Deutero-Isaiah played an important role for the Christian community's interpretation of Jesus' person and fate (even if it is surprising how seldom the conception of Jesus' atoning death is connected with Isaiah 53). It is therefore far from certain that Jesus himself construed his calling and fate in the light of the Servant Songs. Neither Mark 10:45 nor Luke 22:37 (the only sayings of Jesus referring to Isaiah 53) belong to those sayings of Jesus for which authenticity can be claimed with any certainty.

It is not easy to answer the question of whether or not the eschatological figures in Jewish conceptions of the last times derived some features from the Servant. While it is relatively certain that some sayings about the Servant were understood of the Messiah, it is more difficult to decide whether or not they led to modifications in the image of the Messiah. To the question of whether the Jews identified the Messiah (or some other eschatological figure) with the Servant in such a way that the figure of the Messiah received a new configuration, Sigmund Mowinckel, an influential Norwegian Old Testament scholar, responded emphatically in the negative. Yet Mowinckel held open the possibility that in certain Jewish circles the Servant might have stimulated the formation of a new idea of a savior who would come instead of the traditional Messiah, even though nothing of the sort can be demonstrated from the sources. Mowinckel cited the whole paraphrastic revision of Isaiah 53 in the Aramaic Targum (translation), as striking evidence that the scribes were prepared to put the Messiah in place of the Servant without altering the conception of the former. The text was so thoroughly reinterpreted that there is no longer a Servant-Messiah who is portrayed as an abject, suffering figure who suffers an ignominious death. Such sayings are interpreted either of his enemies who will be crushed, or of Israel, who has suffered in the past. It is, accordingly, the picture of the Servant which is adjusted to the conception of the Messiah, and not the reverse.[5]

While there are countless examples of the fact that the rabbis managed to understand biblical passages in ways entirely different from their natural meaning, it is hardly possible to find parallels to the sustained distortion of the text reflected in the Targum to Isaiah 53. This can probably be connected with the fact that the rabbis wanted to contradict and oppose the Christian utilization of the text. But why should they identify the Servant with the Messiah at all? Would it not have been much simpler to understand the Servant as a figure from the remote past or as a symbol of Israel? We can only wonder whether an earlier form of the Targum to Isaiah 53 existed in which the Servant was understood as the Messiah *without* explaining away everything said about his suffering. Had there been a firm tradition that the Servant was the Messiah, it could not be avoided that some of those who read the text in the original Hebrew (and Jesus was one), understood it more or less literally so that they actually became convinced that the Scriptures predicted that the Messiah must suffer and die. In later rabbinic traditions, at any rate, we have evidence for the use of Isaiah 53 as proof for the notion that the Messiah would suffer before being called to his task. That the Servant was "smitten by God" (Isa. 53:4), for example, led to the idea that the Messiah was a leper (in accordance with a widespread understanding of the idiom). The Targumic text certainly witnesses to the extraordinary interpretive skills of the rabbis, particularly in averting a potentially dangerous use of a biblical text. But it does not prove that Isaiah 53 had no influence whatsoever on the messianic ideal in Jewish circles. On the other hand, it must be granted that such an influence can hardly be proved. It is an undemonstrable conjecture to suggest that Isaiah 53 could have inspired the notion of a kind of preliminary Messiah, a "military Messiah" of the tribe of Joseph (or Ephraim), who falls in the war of liberation before the leadership is taken over by the Messiah of Judah. This idea is not attested in sources earlier than the Christian era (e.g., the Jerusalem Targum to Exod. 40:11), and perhaps has a background in such actual historical events as the fate of Bar Kosiba,[6] in the second Jewish revolt (A.D. 132–135).

There is, nevertheless, a more secure basis for claiming that the portrait of the Servant, particularly in Isaiah 53, has contributed to a revision of the image of the ideal martyr and the figure of the suffering righteous one whom we meet in documents such as 2 and 4 Maccabees and the Wisdom of Solomon, and which has a historical tie with the persecution and martyrdom of the Hasidim during the attempt of the Greco-Syrian king Antiochus IV (died 164 B.C.) to Hellenize the Jewish people by force. The depiction of the humiliation and martyrdom of the righteous one and his elevation after death in Wisdom of Solomon 2–5 can very well have affected the gospel narratives of the death of Jesus. It is also interesting that the righteous teacher at Qumran has traits in common with the suffering righteous one, even if it is uncertain whether or not he actually suffered martyrdom.

Of primary importance in this context is the fact that when there are the rudiments of a doctrine that the lot of the righteous in this world entails *suffering,* ideal eschatological figures can scarcely avoid being characterized by this conception. If Isaiah 53 is read as an ideal portrait of the suffering righteous ones, a decisive influence is necessarily exerted on *all* ideal religious figures. There is abundant documentation for the popular conception that religious leaders must necessarily undergo severe testing and experience great persecution. The faith of Abraham was popularly thought to be based on ten difficult tests. Similar stories were told of Joseph. The story of Moses in Egypt and in the wilderness contains many examples of testing. That the prophets all suffered martyrdom was a conception which recurs, even though it cannot be documented from the Scriptures (cf. Matt. 5:12; 23:29-37; Luke 13:33f.). The curious passage in Revelation 11 about the two witnesses apparently presupposes the notion that even Elijah and Moses will suffer martyrdom in connection with the persecutions of the last days! In late rabbinic exegesis, Isaiah 53 is used as evidence that the Messiah was charged with enduring a considerable share of the suffering of the world.

There are two themes which are part of the conception of the sufferings of the righteous one. First, suffering can belong to the preparatory tests which holy people must undergo to be qualified for their God-given calling. That is the theme most easily connected with the Messiah. We find it in the tradition about Jesus in the form of the myth of the temptation in the wilderness. Second, suffering is often regarded as a major element in the mission itself; the righteous one is *called* to suffer. His activities culminate in martyrdom, and that qualifies him for a share in the resurrection of the righteous and exaltation after death. The idea of atonement can also come in at this point, either in the form that the righteous one is permitted to atone for personal sins, thereby avoiding the judgment which will befall everyone else, or as a substitutional atonement for the benefit of others (i.e., Israel). If the Messiah is regarded as sinless, the possibility that his suffering serves as an atonement for his own sin is excluded. These themes, while they occur in the New Testament primarily in connection with Jesus, are also used in connection with his followers.

Since the Jewish evidence is scattered and extremely complex, we must always ask whether support is found in the New Testament, either in that which is reported about Jews or in themes taken over from Judaism by Christians.

The impact of eschatological figures on the New Testament

The New Testament provides confirmation that the Prophet, Elijah, and the Messiah were part of popular eschatological expectations of persons who would come as emissaries of God in the last days. The idea of the Prophet, originally based on Deuteronomy 18, appears only sporadically. Elijah plays a much more prominent role. The Messiah, however, is completely dominant and is the only eschatological figure mentioned in the New Testament epistolary literature. It may appear surprising that the Prophet retreats into the background, since Jesus is expressly identified with the one to whom God refers in statements about the prophet like Moses (Acts 3:22; cf. John 6:14). At least a partial explanation lies in the fact that the theme was relatively unstressed even in Jewish conceptions (as distinct from Samaritan conceptions). In certain Jewish-Christian settings, it appears that the title played a much more prominent role.[7]

In the New Testament, Elijah plays the role of a forerunner of the Messiah and is identified with John the Baptist. Through this understanding, the indirect identification of Jesus with the Messiah is strengthened. But there is also the problem of whether Jesus himself was ever understood as Elijah.

Completely, or at least partially, independent of the prophecies of an eschatological return, the traditions concerning Moses and the Exodus and concerning Elijah (and Elisha as well) have influenced the portrait of Jesus in gospel tradition. As typological anticipations of the Messiah, Moses and Elijah play a more important role in the Gospels than David, even though the Messiah is the son of David. Jesus has little more in common with David than a royal title and a common birthplace in Bethlehem. Even the latter has nothing to do with typology; it is simply the messianic utilization of Mic. 5:1 (Matt. 2:5f.), which makes it necessary to have Jesus of Nazareth born in David's city (Luke 2:4). It is probable that the Fourth Evangelist believed that Jesus personally combined the roles of the Prophet, Elijah, and the Messiah. According to John, he is the fulfillment of all expectations of salvation. Otherwise it is simply not true that the use of Moses and Elijah as typological anticipations in any way implies the identification of Jesus either with Moses *redivivus* or the coming Elijah. It is certainly clear in John 6:14 that the miracle of the loaves is associated with the miracle of manna in such a way that Jesus is revealed as the Prophet (though certainly not a prophet like Moses but, so to speak, the true Moses, the one who really gives people bread from heaven). Similarly, it is possible that Matthew intended that the Sermon on the Mount present Jesus as the new Moses. In and of itself it is probably not so important that it was specifically Moses who was involved in the miracle of manna, to which the miracle of loaves was seen as a higher fulfillment. In the case of the miracle of loaves, there is a far more striking parallel in a relatively neglected tale about how Elisha miraculously multiplied loaves in 2 Kings 4:42-44 (cf. the tale told of Elijah in 1 Kings 17). Jesus' resuscitation of the widow's son at Nain (Luke 7:11-17) is similarly reminiscent of resuscitations performed by Elijah and Elisha (1 Kings 17:17-24; 2 Kings 4:31-36). Several other examples could be mentioned. In part we are dealing with typical miracle stories containing themes which tend to be associated with prophets and holy people (in the Hellenistic world as well). It was also thought appropriate by those who believed that Jesus was the Savior promised in the Scriptures to attribute to him deeds which surpassed those of all others.

Scholars have sometimes regarded it as problematic that Jesus, precisely as the Messiah, should be a wonder-worker, or that miracles should play a role in demonstrating that he was the Messiah,

since the performance of miracles was not part of the Jewish conception of the Messiah's function. The problem is actually quite
artificial. It is true that the Messiah was not regarded as a wonder-
worker in such a way that the claim of messiahship had to be legitimated by the performance of miracles. Apparently this contra-
dicts the gospel accounts that even the Pharisees insisted that Jesus
legitimate himself by a sign from heaven (Mark 8:11 and par.). But
it is also mentioned that some believed that John the Baptist could
be the Messiah (Luke 3:15), and he was certainly no miracle worker.
Rabbi Akiba proclaimed Simon bar Kosiba as the Messiah; neither
was he known for his supernatural abilities. For that matter, there
was no proviso that the Messiah had to perform miracles. But it
certainly would be no great disadvantage if he could! The demand
for legitimation must be viewed in a broader context. Miracles could
hardly legitimate someone as the Messiah, at any rate not unless
those concerned had openly claimed such abilities and had obligated
themselves to demonstrate their claim by a miracle. Josephus tells
of some messianic prophets who promised miracles similar to those
done by Moses and Joshua. Yet miracles could serve as signs that
"God was with him," as it says in Acts 10:38; cf. John 9:16-17,31-
33. The only miracle which proved that Jesus was the Messiah for
Christians was his resurrection, and that is tied to the fact that he
was condemned by the Sanhedrin and Pilate as a messianic pretender.

It is somewhat surprising that the miracle stories told of Jesus
should encourage people to think that he might be the Messiah. To
that we must reply, first, that Jesus was not *only* a miracle worker.
In his mission, miracles were certainly not unimportant, but they
were clearly secondary. Of primary importance was his message that
the kingdom of God was near, and it was mainly this proclamation
which provoked the question of messiahship. Several scholars have
proposed the view that the typological pattern for the Messiah was,
appropriately enough, not David so much as David's *son*—the precise designation ascribed to Jesus several times in connection with
healing miracles.[8] The son and successor to the throne of David was
Solomon. In popular Jewish conceptions, Solomon's wisdom implied insight into all secrets so that he knew how all diseases could
be cured and especially that he had control over demons. The miracles of Jesus consisted primarily of healing and exorcisms. A saying
of Jesus is preserved regarding how he compared himself with the

wise Solomon (Matt. 12:42; Luke 11:31), but it is hardly possible to produce any adequate proof that typology involving Solomon exerted a decisive influence on the Jesus traditions. All the same, there is an indirect basis for thinking that Solomon (who was the only "great" king in Israel's history) exerted a strong influence on the Jewish image of the ideal king and consequently on messianic speculation as well. There is particular reason for considering such an influence at a time and setting in which Wisdom tended to be not only the highest virtue, but was also raised to a divine hypostasis which was extolled and adored.

For the messianic ideal, it is also significant for David as well as for Solomon that, since they were regarded as authors of psalms and wisdom sayings, they were considered prophets (cf. Acts 1:16; 2:30; 4:25; and the use of Psalms and Proverbs as "God's word"). In Qumran and other circles which tended to divide messianic functions between the king and the priest, it was naturally the priest who exercised the prophetic task of interpreting the will of God. But where the kingly Messiah alone is found, it naturally follows that he is the one who possessed inspired wisdom and taught people the proper understanding of God's will. In John 4:25 (placed, to be sure, in the mouth of a Samaritan woman) we read, "I know that Messiah is coming (he who is called Christ); when he comes, he will show us all things." In this respect he surpasses every prophet (cf. John 4:19). That the Messiah is a teacher, preacher, and interpreter of the divine Torah does not in any way contradict the basic conception of the royal Messiah. In Hellenistic Judaism (i.e., Philo of Alexandria), the royal title is readily spiritualized in such a way that the wisest and most virtuous person is also the one with the greatest claim to be called "king." We can detect certain tendencies in this direction within the New Testament as well (e.g., Heb. 7:1-2; 1 Cor. 4:8), most importantly in John 18:36f., where the kingship of Jesus is interpreted spiritually. His kingdom is not of this world. He is king by virtue of his testimony for the truth. He is, even if the expression is never used, king in the kingdom of truth. But such spiritualization of the messianic role is not characteristic of the New Testament as a whole.

Yet one can, properly enough, speak of an essential modification or transformation (which should not be labeled "spiritualization"), for which Paul certainly has primary responsibility. It is based on the premises of Jewish apocalyptic, which gave eschatology cosmic dimensions. In the Pauline letters we find little indication that the titles *Christ* and *Messiah* mean "king of the Jews" (a fact particularly emphasized in John 18:33f.; 19:19). In Paul he is the one who conquers sin and death and cosmic powers. Actually, *Christ* does not function as a title in Paul, but rather as a name for Jesus. The title *kyrios* ("Lord") takes over instead. But, especially in 1 Cor. 15:24-28, the royal theme is used in a way which clearly indicates that Paul is familiar with the apocalyptic conception of a thousand-year kingdom. On the basis of Psalm 110 (the whole of which is a text of fundamental importance for Christology), Paul concludes that Jesus will be king until he has subjected the last enemy to God (or God has subjected the last enemy to him). When that happens (and the last enemy conquered is death), Jesus will give the authority back to God, that he "may be everything to everyone" (1 Cor. 15:28). That Jesus is king implies for Paul, not a blissful state of peace, as for example in the conception, of Rev. 20:1-6, of the thousand years when Satan is chained, but a ceaseless struggle against all forces hostile to God. That probably means that Jesus' kingdom, that time when he has supreme command over the heavenly armies (and over his warriors on earth as well), virtually coincides with the time of the church. That lasts from his resurrection to the day of judgment. In 1 Corinthians 15, however, there are little more than vague hints, but it appears that there has been a marked development from the fairly complex apocalyptic scenario in 2 Thess. 2:5-12, where Jesus at his coming will annihilate the "lawless one," Antichrist, Satan's servant and representative upon the earth. If we decode the figurative language of apocalyptic, the "lawless one" can stand for an actual historical individual, such as Antiochus IV in his day or emperors such as Nero and Domitian in theirs. What is new in relation to Jewish eschatology is the fact that the Messiah is identified with the resurrected Jesus, and that the elect people are identical with the church.

The Revelation of John is the clearest example that Jewish apocalyptic eschatology was taken over and Christianized in this manner. Through his martyrdom, Jesus had shown himself worthy to be resurrected and installed as Messiah. In the fullness of time he will inaugurate God's vengeance upon Satan and his servant on the earth. Here we also meet the characteristic doubling of apocalyptic themes, due to the combination of an originally this-worldly, nationalistic idea of the restoration of David's kingdom with the idea of the destruction of this evil world and the establishment of an entirely new paradisiacal world. The Revelation of John shows how Jesus, on the basis of faith in his resurrection, could be absorbed with relative ease into a Jewish apocalyptic scenario. But, from our perspective, that only widens the distance between the historical portrait of Jesus given by the Synoptic evangelists and the Jewish apocalyptic conception of the Messiah. When we turn from Revelation to the Gospels, it appears incomprehensible that anyone could connect messianic expectation to the person of Jesus while he was still living. For Paul and the author of Hebrews, faith in Jesus as the Messiah led to a new Christology which was defined by the fact that even the messianic mission, so to speak, consists of and is almost exhausted by (and here the Fourth Gospel takes the matter even further) the self-abandonment represented by the crucifixion. To identify the Messiah with Jesus implies that all conceptions of the Messiah must be revised in a way thoroughly offensive to Jews (1 Cor. 1:23).

In the New Testament letters and in Revelation, the identification of Jesus with the Messiah is assumed. The authors had no problem at all in making this identification, even though they knew how problematic it must have been for Jews. They wrote for Christian readers and did not need arguments to prove that Jesus was the Messiah, as was necessary in evangelistic preaching and as was done in later apologetic literature (e.g., Justin Martyr). When, on the other hand, we consider the synoptic Gospels and Acts, we notice that even though they were written much later than the Pauline letters, they reflect an earlier stage of Christological development. Though the answer is never uncertain for the evangelists themselves, they nevertheless lead us directly into the discussion and the dispute regarding the identity of Jesus. That applies in a distinctive way to the Gospel of John as well, where the dispute is stylized and given a theological perspective which creates a greater distance from the historical setting. In these documents Jesus is confronted with *Jewish* conceptions and expectations. Here *Christ* is synonymous with *the Messiah* for whom the Jews waited, even though Jesus differed from the Messiah they had expected. It is also here that we can still find alternatives to *Messiah*.

While the confession of Jesus as the Messiah is fundamental for all Christians, there are nuances. Among other things, there seems to be a more or less pronounced tendency to make the phrase *Son of God* into the most important way of understanding the term *Messiah* and even to use it as an actual title, not only in John but also in Mark and Matthew (cf. Mark 1:1, 11; 15:39; Matt. 16:16; 28:19). There was an excellent biblical basis for calling the Messiah the son of God (2 Sam. 7:14; Ps. 2:7). For a Jew, *son of God* was a symbolic expression describing the special covenant relationship between Yahweh and his anointed one. As an independent messianic title, however, it was rarely used. That has an obvious explanation in efforts to emphasize pure monotheism in a world in which other peoples recognized families of gods and even spoke of physical descent from the gods. The Christian use of the title *Son of God* for Jesus was derived from Judaism. This is evident from the account of the baptism of Jesus, where the heavenly voice, which explains that Jesus is the Son of God, functions exactly like the adoption formula in the royal coronation hymn in Ps. 2:7. "God's son" is formally synonymous with the "Lord's anointed," though the two expressions did not develop precisely the same associations. The latter is tied primarily to the people of Israel; the Messiah is the king of the *Jews. God's son,* however, developed connotations suggesting the close relationship between God and an elect individual. It is an expression of mutual affection and confidence as well as unconditional filial obedience and compliance. In this connection it is important to remember that it is not only the king who is called God's son in the Old Testament and in Jewish literature, but also Israel (when the plural is used, individual Israelites are in view). Particularly meaningful is the tendency in wisdom literature for a personal application of the term to the individual pious person, the righteous one who, so to speak, himself has selected God as his Father, to submit to him in unconditional obedience and boundless confidence.

It can hardly be accidental that we encounter clear echoes in the New Testament from Wis. 1:16—3:9; 4:7—5:23. Also, the similarity between Wisdom of Solomon 5 and Isaiah 53 is certainly intentional. Here we learn how the ungodly make the righteous an object of hatred and mock him because he says that God is his Father and he is God's son. They test his faith by torturing him to death, "for if the righteous man is God's son, he will help him, and will deliver him from the hand of his adversaries" (Wis. 2:18; cf. Matt.

27:43). But the ungodly are shortsighted fools, who do not understand that it is an expression of God's love to deliver young innocents from this ungodly world and take them home to himself in eternal, heavenly joy. They do not think about the just punishment the ungodly themselves shall reap when it will eventually be revealed that the righteous were innocent and their very righteousness becomes an indictment against those who acted unjustly. A point of connection to the theme of the king as God's son can also be present when it is said that the righteous, after having experienced testing, will step forth in all their radiance and "will govern nations and rule over peoples" (Wis. 3:8; cf. Sir. 4:15; 1 Cor. 6:2; Rev. 2:26f.).

God's son is clearly a designation which can have many quite divergent associations, and in individual cases this ambiguity is exploited, even though the basis for applying it to Jesus is primarily its messianic significance. For example, in Mark 15:39, a pagan military officer comments on Jesus' death with the words, "Truly this man was the Son of God" (or, "a son of God"). Luke 23:47 has replaced the phrase "Son of God" with "innocent": "Certainly this man was innocent!" It is worth noting that although the title can be the most presumptuous of all (cf. the high priest's question at Jesus' interrogation in Mark 14:61 par.; cf. also John 5:18: "he makes himself equal with God"), it can also be an expression of humble piety simply to want to be a "child of God" (as presupposed in Wis. 2:13; see also 1 John 3:1 and other passages where the expression is applied to believers). The inference from the notion of the virginal conception in the infancy narratives of Matthew and Luke reveals that the Jewish anxiety that the title could pose a threat to pure monotheism was justified. It was widely applied to express a metaphysical relation which transforms Jesus into a divine being.

For Matthew, who emphasized the title *Son of God* more prominently than Mark and also used the notion of the miraculous conception (Matt. 1:18), there is a kind of spiritualization of the messianic idea. It is clear enough that, for Matthew, *Messiah* means "king" (13:41; 19:28; 20:21; 25:34), yet the national and political aspects are softened. This is not so clear when it says in Matt. 1:21 that the child will be called "Jesus, for he will save his people from their sins," for the Jews could well say something similar about their Messiah. But when the gospel ends with the command of the risen Jesus to go out and make all people disciples of Jesus because he has received all power in heaven and on earth, it is quite clear that we are dealing with a kingdom which is not of this world (even if we must be somewhat cautious in saying that it has a purely "spiritual" character).

Luke in particular is distinguished by a conscious and carefully defined utilization of themes from Jewish messianic ideology. Throughout both the gospel and Acts he makes a contribution toward illuminating Jewish expectations. Surprisingly, he presents Jesus as the fulfillment of those expectations without any reservations. Jesus is none other than the Messiah which God had prepared for the Jewish people (Acts 3:20). Luke 1–2 occupies a relatively unique position; here John and Jesus are linked to one another through parallel legends of miraculous birth within a very Jewish atmosphere. The announcement of the angel to Zechariah (1:13-17) states that John will fulfill all the expectations associated with the returning Elijah. Correspondingly, Gabriel's message to Mary is expressed in the pure style of a classical messianic oracle:

> He will be great, and will be called the Son of the Most High;
> and the Lord God will give to him the throne of his father David,
> and he will reign over the house of Jacob for ever;
> and of his kingdom there will be no end.
>
> (1:32-33)

The allusion to the prophecy of Nathan in 2 Samuel 7 is obvious. (At Qumran, an Aramaic fragment has been found, the word order of which closely corresponds to v. 32a; perhaps it too is a fragment of a messianic prophecy.)[9]

Concerning the Messiah who will be born, Mary's Magnificat says that he will turn the prevailing order upside down by breaking down the proud, overthrowing the mighty, exalting the humble, rejecting the rich, and showing mercy to the descendants of Abraham (1:51-55).

Zechariah's song of praise consists of two parts. The first (1:68-75) concerns the Messiah, while the second (1:76-79) is directly applied to John the forerunner. The Messiah is Israel's redeemer and savior, the promised son of David who liberates his people from their enemies and restores the covenant with the fathers. John is the prophet of the Most High who will go before the Messiah (the Lord) and prepare the way for him. He will preach salvation and forgiveness of sins for his people and lead them into the way of peace.

An angel announced to the shepherds that a Savior was born for them, the Messiah, the Lord, in the city of David. The following song of praise hails him as the prince of peace (2:10-14). The poetic elements sound like excerpts from the royal psalms and appear to be translations from a Hebrew or Aramaic source. There is not a single word which does not correspond to traditional themes concerning Elijah and the Messiah. The Messiah is the new David, Israel's redeemer, the renewer of the covenant, the enforcer of justice, and the protector of the weak.

Even though the infancy legends are relatively self-contained and probably derived from preexisting sources, there are corresponding messianic themes which permeate the rest of Luke and Acts. This occurs most clearly in passages which express the expectations of the disciples prior to their experience of the miraculous day of Pentecost, but without being corrected and revised in later versions of the proclamation of the early community. There is really no difference between the testimony of the disciples on the road to Emmaus in Luke 24:19ff., and Peter's message in Acts (e.g., 10:36-43). The Emmaus disciples were not reproved for having harbored wrong hopes about Jesus, but for lacking faith and for not understanding that the whole life of Jesus corresponded to that which the prophets had predicted regarding the Messiah. He was actually "the one to redeem Israel" (Luke 24:21). Luke 19:11 states that when the disciples were on the way to Jerusalem, they believed that the kingdom of God would very soon be revealed. In Acts 1:6, they say to the risen Jesus: "Lord, will you at this time [cf. v. 4] restore the kingdom to Israel?" None of these passages disputes the fact that it was his task to restore Israel. The correction of the disciples' misconceptions consists only in the instruction that the Messiah first had to experience suffering and death before he could enter into his glory (Luke 24:20), and that no one knows God's hour, something they themselves ought to have realized on the basis of Moses and the Prophets. Quite naturally, Luke is expressing a particularly Christian perspective, despite the references to the Scriptures. Luke only confirms the fact that suffering and death had no place in Jewish conceptions of the Messiah. But, according to Luke, suffering and death had a preparatory significance. It was the first test Jesus had to experience to be legitimately elevated to the position of Lord and Messiah. That means that Jesus during his life on earth was *messias designatus,* the "Messiah elect," the one designated to *become* the Messiah through death and resurrection. As far as we know, it was a novel idea that the Messiah could be one who had experienced death; nevertheless, certain Jewish conceptions indicate that such an idea might not be totally foreign. It appears that people thought that the Prophet of the end time would be Moses himself, or that the Messiah would actually be the resurrected David. Mark 8:28 (and par.) indicates that people thought that Jesus was Elijah (who, to be sure, had not experienced death), or another of the ancient prophets, or even John the Baptist, who himself had suffered martyrdom. (What the latter means is unclear; perhaps the thought was that John the Baptist's spirit had taken up a new residence in Jesus, cf. 2 Kings 2:9,15.) Acts 3:18-26 provides an excellent example of how suffering could fit in with Jewish messianic expectations:

> But what God foretold by the mouth of all the prophets, that his Christ should suffer, he thus fulfilled. Repent therefore, and turn again, that your sins may be blotted out, that times of refreshing may come from the presence of the Lord, and that he may send the Christ appointed for you, Jesus, whom heaven must receive until the time for establishing all that God spoke by the mouth of his holy prophets of old. Moses said, "The Lord God will raise up for you a prophet from your brethren as he raised me up. You shall listen to him in whatever he tells you. And it shall be that every soul that does not listen to that prophet shall be destroyed from the people." And all the prophets who have spoken, from Samuel and those who came afterwards, also proclaimed these days. You are the sons of the prophets and of the covenant which God gave to your fathers, saying to Abraham, "And in your posterity shall all the families of the earth be blessed." God, having raised up his servant, sent him to you first, to bless you in turning every one of you from your wickedness.

Here the titles *Messiah, Prophet,* and *Servant of God* are combined, but in such a way that it is unclear exactly at which point in time they become applicable to Jesus. Was it during his earthly life, as *messias designatus,* that Jesus appeared as God's Servant and played the role of the Prophet? Or, on the other hand, did he come simultaneously as the Messiah and the Prophet? "God, having raised up his servant, sent him to you first" (Acts 3:26) can only apply to the earthly coming of Jesus. The unclarity of the text arises from the fact that it is still Jesus who presently speaks to the Jews through the apostles. Those who did not hear the "Prophet" when he himself spoke still have the possibility of doing so if they now repent when they hear his apostles. It is most remarkable that it is said regarding the parousia of Jesus that he is "the Christ appointed for you" (v. 20), and that it is maintained that the promises apply above all to the Jews (v. 25). This last point is frequently emphasized (2:38; 13:26,32f.,38), and at the same time Jewish responsibility for the death of Jesus is mitigated. It is not easy to see how Luke can combine the positive view of Israel's salvation with the historical fact that the Jews, for the most part, rejected the proclamation of the apostles. It was also thought in accordance with the plan of God that the offer should be transferred to the Gentiles (28:25-28). It is difficult to understand how Luke actually conceptualized the eschatological consummation upon Jesus' return as Israel's Messiah; but somehow or other he certainly must have tied the idea of the restoration of Israel to the small Jewish community. Otherwise, all the nationalistic and political themes in Jewish messianism have quietly disappeared, despite Luke's use of the infancy legends. The dominant impression of Luke 1–2 is almost idyllic, characterized by joy over the birth of the Prince of Peace. This impression is particularly evident in the words of the aged Simeon (Luke 2:30-32): "for mine eyes have seen thy salvation, which thou hast prepared in the presence of all peoples, a light for revelation to the Gentiles, and for glory to thy people Israel." The problem is the implication of the term *salvation*. The Messiah is the Savior. But is salvation the liberation of Israel from pagan domination, or being present with Jesus in paradise? Ambiguity and unclarity on this matter are hardly unique to Luke. This arose unavoidably when belief in the resurrection caught on at the time of the Maccabees and was intensified through apocalyptic dualism which could not find room within this world for final and complete salvation. The tension between this-worldly and otherworldly eschatology in Luke is obvious to us, but it does not seem to have been apparent to him. And where did Jesus stand on this question?

6

Jesus and the Eschatological Roles

The apostolic witness proclaimed Jesus as the Messiah. It was simply assumed that he himself was certain of his messianic calling. Nevertheless, there is an obvious tension in the gospel tradition, a "messianic secret" which is presented with different nuances in the various gospels. Even the Gospel of John, which presents Jesus as making an unambiguous claim to be the Messiah, presents the matter in such a way that the question of who Jesus really is remains undecided the whole time and elicits controversy and doubt. The Fourth Gospel was written to bring about belief that Jesus is the Christ, the Son of God, but also with a consciousness that such a belief is not an option for everyone. At its most profound level, belief was impossible before the resurrection and thereafter could only be created by the Spirit of God. At the same time, unbelief is regarded as self-inflicted, as an expression that people do not want to see what their eyes see or to hear what their ears perceive. All this is set within the earthly ministry of Jesus.

The synoptic Gospels all give the impression that Jesus did not openly identify himself with any of the eschatological figures, whether the Messiah, Elijah, or the Prophet, before the Sanhedrin finally provoked a messianic confession. Yet all these gospels obviously think that Jesus knew all along that he was the Messiah, and that he intended to evoke faith in the disciples that he was such. The question of who Jesus thought he was is much less prominent than in the Gospel of John. At the center stands the proclamation of the coming kingdom of God. It is this gospel which is the object of faith, to the extent that "faith" in Jesus simply means the conviction that what he says is true. The bearer of the message must be trustworthy, but it is the message itself which really counts. The one who bears it is anonymous. By calling himself the "Son of man," Jesus emphasizes precisely that anonymity.

When the Gospels are read critically, one may in fact wonder whether Jesus himself was even the least bit preoccupied with his own person. It may seem as if he was so completely identified with his message that what people thought of him was immaterial, if only they would listen to what he had to say. There are gospel traditions which raise the question of who Jesus was. Yet it is possible to regard these as secondary material which reflects a later setting, since the dispute Christians had with Jews centered on vindicating the view that Jesus was the Messiah. On the other hand, is it historically probable that this question first became pressing only after the death of Jesus?

Two well-defined prophetic figures appeared at about the same time and proclaimed that God's hour had arrived. What the prophets had predicted and the pious had awaited would now be fulfilled. That took place within the context of the general conviction, which had existed for many generations, that the time of the prophets was past and that prophecy would not be reborn until the last days. In that situation one could not avoid asking, Who is this John who cries out that the day of judgment is imminent and invites everyone to submit to his baptism in order to receive forgiveness of their sins? Who is this Jesus who preaches before the people and teaches disciples—without himself having studied—who sets his teaching up against that of the authorities, who drives out demons and heals the sick with simply an authoritative word, who says that the kingdom of God is about to come and invites tax collectors and sinners to enter into it? Who are these two whose appearances are so different but who both demand that all be converted while there is still time?

We repeatedly read in the Gospels that people asked such questions and there is no reason to doubt the fact that they really did. If the principal figures themselves did not perhaps feel any personal need to identify with any specific eschatological role, they could not easily avoid being confronted with questions from people around them, both friends and opponents. Even if the Gospel of John has questionable value as a historical source, we can easily imagine that John the Baptist could be provoked into responding to the kind of questions expressed in John 1:19ff. For that matter, John's answers do not appear at all unreasonable. The Fourth Evangelist has a theological interest in depicting John the Baptist neither as the Messiah, Elijah, nor the Prophet, because he wanted indirectly to suggest that Jesus alone is the fulfillment of all the prophecies, and that he combines in his own person the roles of Messiah, Elijah, and the Prophet. Yet it is historically probable that John the Baptist did not want to be anything other than the anonymous voice in the wilderness. What is reported about his clothing and life-style characterizes him as a prophetic preacher of repentance but, though the evangelists want the readers to be reminded of Elijah (2 Kings 1:8), that is no proof that John himself consciously intended to play the part of Elijah. We know with relative certainty that Jesus was confronted with the question of whether he regarded himself as the Messiah, but responded with an answer very different from that of John. We know this, not only because it is reported by all the Gospels, but also because the entire tradition about the death of Jesus has meaning and coherence only if Jesus was crucified as a messianic pretender.[10]

The evidence which is available to us, on the basis of which we will try to provide the most precise answer possible regarding how Jesus saw his own person in relation to the existing eschatological role models, is extremely varied. There are fairly direct sayings where Jesus takes a position in response to questions regarding his identity. When we look beyond the Gospel of John, the whole issue turns on just three traditions: Jesus' answer to the question from the imprisoned John the Baptist, the episode at Caesarea Philippi where the disciples had to report what they thought of Jesus, and the interrogation of Jesus before the high priest. Related, but judged more likely to be authentic by the method of tradition criticism, are the various pronouncements of Jesus about John the Baptist. They are important, for Jesus can scarcely assign an eschatological role to John without indirectly suggesting what he thought of himself. It will be useful to examine these latter texts first, thus keeping in mind that the question of who Jesus thought he was cannot be asked without taking into consideration that there were *two* individuals who appeared on the scene at about the same time, and that there are several factors which link them to each other.

In the modern scholarly discussion of the problem of Jesus' view of himself, the *indirect* evidence, i.e., the words and deeds of Jesus which reflect a distinctive self-consciousness and understanding of his calling, play a proportionately greater role than direct evidence. In effect, nearly the entire Jesus tradition is included in one way or another. Even though the content of Jesus' preaching is primarily religious and ethical instruction, which is independent of whatever role he plays, it is given a form which nonetheless suggests something about the authority Jesus felt justified in assuming. Clearer evidence is provided by direct pronouncements of Jesus which accompany various situations and activities, such as in connection with exorcisms and healings, the promise of the forgiveness of sins, the violation of Sabbath and purity regulations, deviations from the pious life-style, and the like. The possible symbolic significance of his actions must also be examined, e.g., his selection of 12 disciples, his riding into Jerusalem, his cleansing of the temple, and his introduction of a distinctive ritual at the last supper. Another legitimate question is whether there are features which reflect the fact that he felt that he had a special relationship to God. The tradition is manifold and is certainly open to many interpretations. It may also appear to contain mutually contradictory features, especially in the matter of Jesus' self-evaluation. This is a particularly pressing problem in connection with the use of the self-designation *Son of man*.

Jesus on John the Baptist

Jesus' statements about John the Baptist generally appear to be authentic. Since they give the impression of such a high evaluation of John and provide such a positive assessment of his activity, they cannot reasonably be regarded as having originated with the early church. After Jesus' death, his followers must have very quickly regarded the disciples of John the Baptist as possible competitors who, with misdirected zeal for their prophet, refused to open their eyes to the fact that John was really no more than a forerunner for the Messiah, Jesus. For that matter, it is also possible that the positive view of John the Baptist as the forerunner of Jesus was, so to speak, forced upon Christians by Jesus himself, for that was no obvious way of understanding their relationship, when we consider how dissimilar the two actually were (cf. Matt. 11:16-19).

In Matt. 11:7-18 = Luke 7:24-35, several sayings have been gathered together to form a brief speech about John the Baptist which Jesus ostensibly made after John had been thrown into prison. The setting for the speech is the occasion on which a delegation arrived from John to ask Jesus whether he was the one for whom they were waiting. But the response was not directed to the disciples of John. It is rather directed toward the crowd, which may be presumed to be less vitally interested in the phenomenon of John the Baptist. It had been somewhat fashionable to make a trip to hear and see the strange wilderness preacher, but most people returned shaking their heads. "He's crazy!" they said. Yet Jesus responded in a completely different way. He defended John and declared that he was right. He was a true prophet. More than that, he was that messenger of God of whom it was written that he would prepare the way for the Lord. The biblical passage quoted in Matt. 11:10 = Luke 7:27 alludes to several Old Testament texts, but primarily to the conclusion of Malachi, the last prophetic book. Mark also used it in the redactional opening of his gospel (1:2). It must be considered possible that the biblical citation is secondary, as are many other biblical passages attributed to Jesus, yet it does fit the situation particularly well. That Jesus thought of the text from Malachi in connection with John is confirmed by a saying which will be discussed below. Jesus continues the speech by saying that no woman has ever given birth to anyone greater than John. But to this is appended a striking reservation which is not very easy to interpret:[11] "yet he who is least in the kingdom of God is greater than he" (Luke 7:28; cf. Matt. 11:11).

This saying *seems* to imply that John, despite his importance, is still outside the kingdom of God. To exclude him from the kingdom of God, however, cannot be its meaning. Rather, the saying makes sense if it is understood as a response to the future: all who are in the coming kingdom of God are "greater" than John is at present. To be the greatest of prophets is less than to have a place in the kingdom to come. An underlying thought may be that the fulfillment exceeds the prophecy (cf. Luke 16:16).

Matthew 11:12-15 exhibits several tradition-critical and exegetical problems which would take much too long to discuss. This one point is clear, however, that John signals a major turning point in history. The time of prophecy is over and the struggle over the kingdom of God is on. In this connection, Jesus says unambiguously that John is Elijah. Since it is likely that v. 14 derives from the tradition found in Mark 9:11-13 = Matt. 17:10-13, we will not discuss this further at this point.

The speech concludes, in both Matthew (11:16-19) and Luke (7:31-35), with a parable comparing the people with children playing in the marketplace. The point is usually understood to be that the people resemble lazy youngsters who will not join the games, either playing funeral, as John did, or playing wedding, as Jesus has done (cf. Mark 2:19, par.). However, the wording is better suited to a convincing interpretation proposed by Olof Linton:[12] The adversaries complain that John will not celebrate and Jesus will not fast. Both differ in distinctive ways, the one with his ascetic gravity, the other with his frivolity. We need not take a position on either exegetical alternative, since the point is the same in both cases. The adversaries, with their critical attitude, exclude themselves. In their eyes neither John nor Jesus is acceptable, and consequently they miss out on that which God offers them through his two messengers. The characteristics of the two are extremely interesting, from a historical perspective. For us the most important matter is that Jesus, even though he had a keen eye for contrast, takes a firm stand beside John. Both are sent by the same God. If the critics, who know so well what is right, had really been clever, then they would have both mourned with John and rejoiced with Jesus.

Another passage in which Jesus connects his ministry with that of John functions as part of the prelude to the passion narrative (Mark 11:27-33 = Matt. 21:23-27 = Luke 20:1-8). Members of the Sanhedrin wanted to know what right Jesus had to act as he did, probably with reference to the so-called cleansing of the temple (Mark 11:15-17, par.). Jesus did not respond directly, but first demanded to hear their view of John, whether they thought that he performed his baptism with divine authority or whether it was merely of human origin. If they would first answer that question, then he would reveal the source of his own authority. The members of the Sanhedrin were in a predicament. They could not very well say that the baptism of John was from God, since they had not submitted to it themselves. They were afraid to say the opposite in order not to provoke the wrath of the people, who regarded John as a true prophet. Consequently, they replied, "We do not know." Thereupon Jesus refused to answer their question. What stands out clearly, if indirectly, is that Jesus actually claimed the same right to do what he did as John claimed in instituting his baptism. Matthew includes a continuation in which Jesus attacks the leaders of the people because they did not want to listen to John (Matt. 21:28-32). "For John came to you in the way of righteousness, and you did not believe him" (Matt. 21:32). It appears from Jesus' statements that he considered his own ministry as a *continuation* of that of John, not as an *alternative* to it. That presupposes historically that Jesus primarily found support among the same people whom John had influenced. That did not mean, however, that all the disciples of Jesus had experienced baptism or that all the followers of John later associated themselves with Jesus. Yet the text does not reflect the problem which the Christian community later had to face when the disciples of John did not want to recognize Jesus as the Messiah.

In this connection we must consider Mark 9:11-13 and Matt. 17:10-13, where we have the peculiar situation that the wording is logical and clear in Matthew, while his alleged source, Mark, has a confused text which exhibits no reasonable coherence.[13] It is assumed that even though John was regarded as a prophet by many, he was not identified with the eschatological Elijah. Jesus was the first to do that. Even though the purpose was primarily to announce the nearness of the kingdom of God (the forerunner has already performed his task), it appears inescapable that the disciples must have understood the saying as an indirect proclamation of messiahship. It is certainly surprising that this is not intimated by the evangelists (cf. Matt. 17:13); but that is perhaps not so remarkable when one remembers that the episodes reported immediately before are those which treat Peter's confession and the transfiguration on the mountain. Against this background it would appear anticlimatic to suggest that the identification of John with Elijah carried with it a suggestion that Jesus must be the Messiah.

That "Elijah must first come" does not automatically mean "before the Messiah," for Malachi 3–4 (to which the phrase refers), does not mention the Messiah. Elijah is the forerunner of *God*. But if the Messiah is to have any place at all in the scheme, it must necessarily be after the forerunner. And since Jesus' disciples understood him to be a prophet greater than John, and John represented

Elijah of the last days, there was no other role that Jesus could play in the eschatological drama than that of the Messiah.

Jesus himself must have thought along very much the same lines. His own self-consciousness could not be completely unaffected by his understanding of John. Among the existing eschatological role models, the idea of a pair of prophets was in fact present. Yet that does not fit the fact that Jesus and John appeared separately. Since there was also a certain interval of time, it is easy to think in terms of the pattern forerunner—successor. And if the one was Elijah, the other must be the Messiah.[14]

Traditions that Jesus claimed to be the Messiah

After having considered his statements regarding John the Baptist, it is appropriate to turn to the account of Jesus' answer to John's question (Matt. 11:2-6 = Luke 7:18-23). John sent a message from prison with some disciples who asked Jesus, "Are you he who is to come, or shall we look for another?" In the light of our discussion of the various figures occurring in eschatological expectations, it is possible that the formula "he who comes" (Greek: *ho erchomenos*), was used to keep all options open. The expression means the one whom God will send at the end, whether Elijah, the Prophet, or the Messiah (or, for that matter, Michael). The evangelists obviously mean the Messiah. The message Jesus sent back with John's disciples corresponded to the suggestive form of the question. The response did not consist in a direct answer but, strictly speaking, refers only to what John already knew previously: "the blind receive their sight and the lame walk, lepers are cleansed and the deaf hear, and the dead are raised up, and the poor have good news preached to them" (Matt. 11:5 = Luke 7:22). To that, Jesus appends a warning, also in indirect form: "And blessed is he who takes no offense at me." In one sense the answer is clear. The one who really comprehends what is happening cannot be in doubt about who Jesus is, for what is taking place is in fulfillment of the prophetic promises. Those familiar with Scripture will be reminded of a series of passages in Isaiah (29:18; 35:5f.; 42:7,18; 26:19; 61:1). None mentions the cleansing of lepers. This feature can be due to the typological influence of the Elijah–Elisha tradition (cf. 2 Kings 5). Exorcisms are not mentioned, probably because they did not belong to biblical prophecies either.

Judgments regarding the historicity of these traditions are difficult. The suggestive and indirect character of both question and answer as well as the silence regarding John's response suggest the genuineness of the tradition. But other features engender doubt. It is apparently assumed that John had earlier believed that Jesus was the one who would come after him, the one who would baptize with fire. What he learned of Jesus' activities caused him to doubt. Modern readers interpret this in the sense that John had awaited a Messiah who would accomplish the judgment of the Lord and that he took offense at what he heard about the "gentle Jesus." It is not at all clear that the evangelists thought along these same lines. They do not suggest a tension between two messianic ideas. But is it historically probable that John regarded Jesus as the Messiah? How could it then be that not *all* of John's disciples became associated with Jesus? The situation can be understood in such a way that it was not until his imprisonment that John, on the basis of what his disciples reported, began to believe that perhaps Jesus might be the one who was to come. But that does not cohere well with the tone of warning in Jesus' final statement. As we will see later, Jesus' answer to John harmonizes well with what we otherwise know about how Jesus understood what happened around him as a sign of the breaking in of the time of salvation. In that respect the tradition appears reliable. Yet, historical criticism raises so many problems that it is inadvisable to base very much on this story. There is therefore no point in asking whether John thought primarily of Elijah or of the Messiah when he asked the question he did.

In the Gospel of Mark, Peter's confession marks both a high point and a turning point in the narrative. The disciples understood that Jesus was the Messiah, and from that point on Jesus began to prepare them for his suffering and death. There is virtually complete agreement among Mark 8:27-30; Luke 9:18-21; and Matt. 16:13-16. The expanded version of the story in Matt. 16:17-19 appears secondary and need not be of major concern. Jesus provoked a confession from the disciples by first asking, "Who do people say that I am?" (RSV, alt.). They expressed various opinions: John the Baptist, Elijah, one of the old prophets (e.g., Jeremiah). According to the structure of the story, none of the answers could be completely satisfactory. This may be the reason why "the Prophet" is not included (cf. John 1:21); it would have been too good an answer. Neither is it justifiable to draw the conclusion that no one had hitherto suspected that Jesus could be the Messiah. The dramatic tension of the account would have been spoiled had the correct response already been mentioned. It could only occur when Jesus asked the disciples directly, "Who do you say that I am?" Peter responded, "You are the Messiah." Even though Jesus did not comment on the answer, but simply imposed an obligation to remain silent on the disciples, it is obviously assumed that this is the right answer. The clever hypothesis of tradition criticism that it was originally Peter's confession which evoked the reaction, "Get behind me, Satan!" (i.e., that Jesus regarded the idea of wanting to be the Messiah as a satanic temptation), is initially alluring, but on reflection appears totally improbable. Yet it is also misleading to maintain, as many do, that Jesus indirectly corrected the disciples' confession by calling himself the Son of man in the following passion prediction, as if the really correct answer should not have been, "You are the Messiah," but, "You are the Son of man." Such an interpretation is obviously meaningless when the Matthean parallel is considered, which expresses Jesus' opening question as, "Who do people say that the Son of man is?" (RSV, alt.). That Peter's conception of the Messiah has to be corrected is quite another matter. The real point in the instruction of the disciples which follows is to prepare the way for the radically new perspective that Jesus must experience suffering and death precisely because he is the Messiah. The following episode with Peter (Mark 8:31-33; Matt. 16:21-23), which Luke omits (possibly because the coarse reprimand of the foremost apostle was less edifying for the evangelist's taste), complements the scene of Peter's confession. That it is far easier to credit Jesus with the sharp reprimand of Peter than a legendary account of the church confirms that we are dealing with historical tradition both with reference to the messianic confession and the passion prediction (even if the description exhibits features of later adaptation to the story of the crucifixion). Whether Jesus also spoke of his resurrection is open to doubt. The reaction of Peter is easier to understand if it had not been mentioned. That does not mean, however, that the resurrection did not pertain to Jesus' own perspective.

There have been many attempts to reconstruct a different historical basis for the gospel tradition of Peter's confession. Yet they are all burdened with greater improbabilities than the account in Mark to the extent that they tend to strengthen faith in the tradition. In appropriate situations the command to silence also has its place. The stereotypical and at times completely inappropriate use of the command to silence, especially in Mark, does not justify believing that we are dealing only with an editorial idea which has no basis in the life of Jesus. If it is historically true that Jesus regarded himself as the Messiah, then the messianic secret must also be historical. The motives for holding this belief by himself, or within a small circle of specially trusted men, are obvious. But it is also evident that "nothing is hidden except to be made manifest" (Mark 4:22). A secret is destined for disclosure when the proper time arrives.

For Jesus, that time came when he stood before the Sanhedrin. We cannot know precisely what transpired or what was said at that impromptu interrogation, which hardly followed proper juridical procedure. The sources are not only problematic, but partly contradictory as well. Luke 22:66-71 is quite different from Mark 14:55-65 and Matt. 26:59-68 (to say nothing of John 18). But they are in agreement on the main issue. What happened is that the leader of the council provoked Jesus into publicly acknowledging that he was the Messiah. To have Jesus executed, it was necessary on the one hand to give the Sanhedrin a basis for condemning him for blasphemy, and on the other hand to provide the Roman authorities a basis for considering him a political revolutionary. The high priest achieved his objective through a two-pronged question, which resulted in Jesus' admission that he was the Son of God in such a way that it could be construed as blasphemy and at the same time acknowledged the title *Messiah* in such a way that he could be denounced before Pilate as the leader of a sedition. The trial of Jesus is a controversial matter which has attracted the attention of Jewish as well as Christian scholars. There is a great deal about it which is unclear or uncertain, but even the indisputable fact that Jesus was crucified as a messianic pretender makes it overwhelmingly probable that he had expressed himself in such a way that it had to be understood as a concession that he was the Messiah. In an important article, Nils A. Dahl has reconstructed this in such a way that one could argue that it was really the opponents of Jesus who forced the title on him.[15] Even though Jesus walked into the trap with open eyes, we get the impression that he was cornered. He had to answer yes to the question of whether or not he was the Messiah because a no would appear to be defection and cowardice. Dahl's argumentation is, in part, psychologically based and for that reason alone problematic. Yet it is difficult for me to understand that his view has any validity at all unless Jesus harbored messianic pretensions and had given his followers a reasonable basis for connecting the messianic call to him. Historical examples can easily be found in which heroic people in life-or-death situations have tolerated false accusations for reasons of a higher loyalty. But if Jesus had thoroughly refused all suggestions that he wanted to be the Messiah and opposed tendencies among his disciples to link messianic expectations to him, it is difficult to find any reasonable basis why he should suddenly reverse himself and declare himself the Messiah before the Sanhedrin, so much more because it could have placed his friends in great danger.

On the other hand, even though he had only implicitly tolerated the fact that the disciples regarded him as the coming Messiah, if he had indirectly contributed to creating such hopes, then it is understandable that he had to show his true colors at the interrogation and acknowledge that he laid claim to the rank of Messiah, even if he could do so only with inner reservations, since the situation did not provide the opportunity for more precisely defining what he meant by *Messiah* or in what sense he thought of himself in that role. While he had been able to instruct the disciples following Peter's confession, the Sanhedrin could only be given a yes, which they had to construe however they wished. The tradition reports, to be sure, that he tried to say something further, but the Gospels give us different versions. While Mark has Jesus respond with an unambiguous "yes," the answer in Matthew and even more in Luke sounds evasive. All three gospels have Jesus add a prophetic saying that the Son of man will sit at the right hand of God, a clear allusion to Ps. 110:1. Mark and Matthew connect it with a saying about his coming with the clouds of heaven, derived from Dan. 7:13. At any rate, the purpose is scarcely to define more closely what kind of Messiah Jesus wanted to be, but rather to give the messianic proclamation a defiant form: this person who now stands bound and helpless before them shall henceforth be enthroned in a place of honor at the right hand of God. The combination of these two messianic texts is doubtless an expression of the biblical interpretation of the early Christian community. If Jesus' reference to Psalm 110 were authentic, it would be of great importance, yet it is not unlikely that these words were only later attributed to him. From a historical perspective, little more can be claimed than that it is highly probable that at the interrogation Jesus answered "yes" to the question of whether or not he was the Messiah. The accusation of blasphemy could have been based either on the fact that he also claimed to be the Son of God, or on the defiant saying that the Son of man—Jesus—would henceforth be enthroned at the right hand of God.

7

Indirect Indications of Jesus' Identity

Technically, the question we have set for ourselves has already been answered: Jesus identified himself as the Messiah. Yet precisely because it has been answered, the inquiry needs to be pursued further. It would have been far less problematical if he simply regarded himself as a prophet or as Elijah or refused any identification with a particular eschatological role. If his own consciousness must be defined as messianic, then we must also see if we cannot define what he meant more precisely. How did he understand his messianic role?

A fundamental problem lies in the fact that Jesus could only admit he was the Messiah in the sense that he had been chosen to *become* the Messiah. He was the *messias designatus,* the "Messiah elect." The real messianic task still lay before him. If he had been anointed as Messiah, he certainly had not been crowned. (An anticipatory anointing was a familiar Old Testament theme; cf. the anointing of David by Samuel in 1 Sam. 16:13, which resulted in the coming of the Spirit of the Lord upon David.) That does not mean that in the interim he must simply wait while preparing himself for his future task as king of Israel. The tension between the present and the future constantly felt in Jesus' proclamation of the kingdom of God was made concrete in his own person. The one who will come already has come, even though he has come in a different manner than he will later come. The one who is called and chosen to become the Messiah is already, in a certain sense, the Messiah. From one perspective one can say that Jesus was his own forerunner. But it is more accurate to focus on the analogy with David, who was anointed by God's prophet long before he assumed his kingdom (cf. the citation of Isaiah 61 in Luke 4:18).

If we could assume that it was based on authentic historical tradition, the report about the "inaugural sermon" of Jesus in Luke 4:16-21 would be an obvious point of departure, since it provides a fairly direct messianic self-testimony. That, however, is precisely what we cannot assume. We are compelled to reach our goal by more circuitous routes.

Now is the time of salvation

There is a series of sayings which indicate in different ways that a new situation has been inaugurated with the coming of Jesus. We can begin with Mark 2:18-20 (and par.). One day someone asked Jesus, "Why do John's disciples and the disciples of the Pharisees fast, but your disciples do not fast?" Jesus replied, "Can the wedding guests fast while the bridegroom is with them?"

That fasting and celebrating are not complementary is easy to understand, since fasting is an expression of sorrow. Fasting was forbidden on the Sabbath, because it was to be a day of rejoicing. The Law prescribed fasting only on the annual day of repentance and prayer, the Day of Atonement (Yom Kippur). Pious Jews such as the Pharisees and (as we learn in Mark 2:18-20) the disciples of John the Baptist fasted voluntarily for as many as two days each week (Luke 18:12). Either this practice represented repentance or was intended to express the continuing sorrow of Israel over the fact that the hand of the Lord lay heavy upon them because of their sins. Jesus and his disciples did not take over their contemporaries' pious practices of fasting. That in itself is an interesting piece of information (cf. Matt. 11:19a). But the reason is even more important. It would have been just as absurd for Jesus' disciples to fast, since they had Jesus with them, as it would have been for the bridegroom's closest friends to do so during the wedding celebration. As long as Jesus was with them, they lived in a state of joy impossible to reconcile with the practice of fasting. This metaphor seems to have been chosen not only because a wedding is the best example of a joyful celebration but also because of the bridegroom's role as the focus of the celebration. (In patriarchal societies he is, even more than the bride, the central figure.) If the continuation in v. 20 is authentic ("The days will come, when the bridegroom is taken away from them, and then they will fast in that day"), Jesus turned the metaphor into an allegory which must be understood as a prediction of his own death and the sorrow which will overtake the disciples. There is no reasonable basis for doubting that Jesus could use allegory in such a way, and the fact that the prediction refers only to his death without hinting at the resurrection suggests that it was not formulated later (cf. John 16:20-22). (The popular theory that v. 20 provides a basis for the introduction of fasting days in the early community has little justification.) The motif of the "marriage of the Lamb" is familiar from Revelation 19, which could suggest that there were extant Jewish metaphors of the Messiah as the bridegroom of Israel and the time of salvation as a marriage celebration. But even if analogous metaphors are familiar from the Old Testament as illustrations of the relationship of Yahweh to Israel, we have no evidence that the "bridegroom" was used as a metaphor for the Messiah. It cannot be assumed that this saying of Jesus would evoke messianic associations. It is not easy to determine how much weight should be placed on this particular use of metaphor. Jesus defended his own disciples (and himself, indirectly, since he did not teach them to fast), but did not reproach those who did practice fasting. That reflects to some extent his loyal attitude toward John the Baptist. But his own person stands firmly in focus as the reason why it is not currently appropriate for his friends to fast. He does not claim that the time for fasting is over, and that now everyone ought to rejoice, but rather: You can fast as much as you wish, but do not expect similar behavior from those who are associated with me! When we consider how life turned out to be so difficult in so many ways for Jesus and his followers (cf. sayings such as Matt. 8:20), Jesus' answer appears almost paradoxically challenging. But it is not unique. "But blessed are your eyes, for they see, and your ears, for they hear. Truly, I say to you, many prophets and righteous men longed to see what you see, and did not see it, and to hear what you hear, and did not hear it" (Matt. 13:16-17 = Luke 10:23-24). This means nothing less than that they have experienced the fulfillment of what Jews had anticipated for centuries, the salvation which the prophets had predicted. The promises are fulfilled in Jesus' proclamation and mighty deeds.

We can also point to such sayings as, "something greater than the temple is here" (Matt. 12:6), or, "something greater than Jonah is here" (Matt. 12:41 = Luke 11:32), or "something greater than Solomon is here" (Luke 11:31 = Matt. 12:42). What can be more holy than the temple? Who can be wiser than Solomon? (The context makes it legitimate to formulate questions such as these. In the case of Jonah the point of comparison is unclear.) The comparison with Jonah at the very least implies a prophetic self-consciousness. That Jesus regarded himself as a prophet is confirmed by Mark 6:4 and par.; Matt. 13:57; Luke 4:24; 13:33. In all these examples the neutral formulation "something greater is here" should be understood personally: "*I* am greater," "*I* am more significant." That can only mean that to Jesus is allotted the most important task in the history of the world.

In the same connection we can adduce expressions such as, "I have come to," which express Jesus' consciousness of possessing a divine commission. Such expressions correspond to phrases such as "I have been sent" in the Gospel of John. All who have a call from God can express themselves in such a manner; such expressions are not unique to Jesus. What is unique emerges only when we consider the basis of the call or commission. All sayings so formulated have been considered a distinctive oral or literary *form*, but that is no argument against their possible authenticity. It is completely arbitrary to deny all sayings of Jesus of the "I have come" type as inauthentic with the argument that they look back on Jesus' work as a whole and therefore are unmasked as sayings spoken by the resurrected one through Christian prophets. (The whole idea that many of the traditional words of Jesus were derived from Christian prophets who expressed the message from the Lord in the first person is based on very weak evidence. For the most part, early Christians clearly distinguished between traditional sayings of Jesus and prophetic sayings of the type found, for example, in Revelation 2–3.) The sayings must be individually evaluated. In my view there are both authentic and inauthentic words of Jesus among the "I have come to . . ." sayings of Jesus, but to decide which is which can be exceedingly difficult.

Among the sayings which appear authentic are the words found in Luke 12:49-51, "I came to cast fire upon the earth; and would that it were already kindled! I have a baptism to be baptized with; and how I am constrained until it is accomplished! [Or: and how I desire that it will be accomplished!] Do you think that I have come to give peace on earth? No, I tell you, but rather division." (Verse 51 corresponds to Matt. 10:34, where "sword" stands in place of "division.") It is difficult to decide the exact meaning of such a metaphorical saying. What does fire symbolize in this case? Jesus has come to set the world on fire. This mode of expression is more suggestive of a fire intentionally set (e.g., with fire arrows), than of spontaneous combustion. But before he can carry out this life-work, he must himself experience a "baptism" and that must also be a "baptism with fire." That certainly hints at martyrdom. This seems to suggest that the death of Jesus would, as it were, become the flame that ignites the world conflagration. It is uncertain whether or not there is any original connection with the sayings that follow about the strife which Jesus will cause, because people will divide themselves in two camps, those for him and those against him. The fire cannot directly correspond to this mutual conflict. But the clear division into two camps can be part of the process. The boundary between those who are on the side of God and those who are on the side of Satan will become clearly marked, and this is the condition for the final, universal judgment. At any rate, such sayings imply that Jesus will play the completely decisive role in the conclusive act of the drama. His death means the arrival of the world's hour of destiny.

We sense a tension between the cosmic perspective and the apocalyptic visions which the image of a world conflagration evokes, on the one hand, and the following description (Luke 12:52f.) of the division of families, on the other. Yet that is perhaps because people of today understand the world from a different perspective. The nature of apocalypticism is such that what for us appear to be insignificant phenomena, limited in extent, assume cosmic proportions. It is doubtful whether we can conclude from a text such as this that Jesus did not regard himself as the Messiah of Israel, but rather as a being with cosmic significance, so to speak, a judge and savior of the world. For a Jew, Israel was God's own people, and Jerusalem was the navel of the earth. In effect, the rest of the universe stood in the background. The point of the expectation of peace spoken of in Luke 12:51 is not the universal state of peace but the *shalom* which will prevail among the liberated and reunited people. Yet the expectations attributed to Jesus in this passage can occasion some surprise. Why was it expected that he should create this peace? Because he preached about forgiveness and reconciliation and love? Because he was a good man who exerted a positive influence? These reasons alone are inadequate. The answer must involve a particular role expectation, a belief that Jesus was the one whom God had sent to restore peace. Specifically, it appears that it must mean that people saw in Jesus either the Prince of Peace himself, the Messiah, or Elijah who would turn the hearts of the fathers to their children. The latter could provide a particularly appropriate background for the following sayings about quarrels within the family.

With regard to this expectation, the question in Matt. 8:29 of the demoniac may be mentioned: "What have you to do with us, O Son of God? Have you come here to torment us before the time?" We will soon see that Jesus could well have responded positively to this question.

There is a saying of a completely different type which also exhibits the "I have come to . . ." structure and takes a stand on the expectations of others, namely, Matt. 5:17, "Think not that I have come to abolish the law and the prophets; I have come not to abolish them but to fulfil them." It is possible that the term translated *fulfil* was as ambiguous in Aramaic as it is in Greek, and that it was intended to suggest several meanings. Since the opposite is "to nullify," "to dissolve," "to abolish," a connotation like "to confirm" or "to make valid" is appropriate. But the term is used in other ways, for example, of fulfilling a command or a prophecy, and it is hardly by chance that it here stands without an object ("them" has no equivalent in the Greek text), even if we can supply "the Law and the Prophets" from what precedes. The program of Jesus does not at all involve dissolving or breaking down. More positively, it involves fulfilling, restoration, completion. In this instance the idea that Jesus had come to abolish the Law and the Prophets is attributed to a particular eschatological role expectation.

There was no Jewish expectation which anticipated the nullification of the Law. To be sure, it is conceivable that the Law would prove superfluous in the messianic era, when everyone would personally fulfill the commandments and there would be no need for atonement or purification, but that does not mean the same thing as abolishing it. The Messiah (or Elijah) will not bring some new law, but the perfect interpretation of the traditional Law, which clarifies everything that had been unclear and disputed. Neither is it true that because Jesus was believed to be the Messiah it was believed that he would abolish the Law, nor can that expectation be claimed for any of his followers. Here the accusations of opponents must be reflected, from people who took offense at Jesus' attitude on such matters as the Sabbath command and the rules for purification. Objections can certainly be raised against accepting the saying as authentic, because it is easy to imagine that Christians, in the subsequent conflict over the validity of the Law, could formulate such statements as this: "Do not think that Jesus came to abolish the law. . . ." It would not be strange if such an explanation was secondarily transformed into a saying of Jesus in the first person.

In several cases similar arguments can be proposed. The saying in Mark 2:17 (and par.), "I came not to call the righteous, but sinners," could be a characteristic statement of Jesus. Yet it could also have originated from a statement about Jesus (in the third person) which was later changed to the first person and attributed directly to him. The content of such sayings will be treated later. Important, yet controversial, is the saying in Mark 10:45 (= Matt. 20:28): "For the Son of man also came not to be served but to serve and to give his life as a ransom for many." In content, this saying corresponds to Luke 22:27 and John 13:4-17, but it is strongly reminiscent of the Christian understanding of the death of Jesus as a propitiatory sacrifice (cf. 1 Tim. 2:6). In fact, we are also reminded of the words of institution at the last supper. The absence of an exact parallel in Luke 22:27 is scarcely a valid argument against the authenticity of this saying. It is far from obvious that the original saying has been preserved in Luke 22:27. If Jesus read Isaiah 53 as a messianic prophecy and understood his own calling on the basis of that passage, he could be credited with these words which are attributed to him. Earlier we argued that behind the thoroughly reworked Targum of Isaiah was an older exegesis which did not interpret away the Servant's (i.e., the Messiah's) suffering and death.

But the indications that Jesus was familiar with such a tradition are conspicuously weak. The citation in Luke 22:37 is not a sufficient basis for such a conclusion. Whether Mark 10:45 ought to be accepted with some probability as an authentic saying of Jesus must remain an open question.

Jesus' comments on exorcism

Among the traditional sayings in which Jesus comments on his own activities, there is a saying about exorcisms which most scholars regard as authentic: "But if it is by the finger [Matthew: Spirit] of God that I cast out demons, then the kingdom of God has come upon you" (Luke 11:20 = Matt. 12:28). The Greek verb *phthanein* actually means "to come upon, overtake," so that the meaning could possibly be that the kingdom of God has already come, or the like (cf. Matt. 8:29), but it is used elsewhere in the New Testament of "to reach, attain." Exorcisms provide a foretaste of the kingdom of God. They even signify that the kingdom of God is already present with such force that the demonic powers must flee. The saying functions as a response to the malicious insinuation from the Pharisaic party that Jesus' power over demons was due to his close connection with Beelzebul, the prince of demons, the evil one himself. Jesus first demonstrates how absurd it is that Satan should cast out Satan. Then comes an ironical observation on Pharisaic exorcists; one would scarcely suggest of them that they derive their authority from the prince of demons. The remark is interesting because it reveals that what Jesus was doing was not unique. Yet at the same time we can be certain that Jesus did not regard the achievements of Pharisaic exorcists as a sign that the kingdom of God had come. That means that also the subject of this saying must be emphasized ("if *I* cast out demons"). The exorcisms cannot be evaluated without regard to their context. They are intimately connected to the whole of Jesus' proclamation of the kingdom of God. In that setting they indicate that Jesus did not simply speak as a prophet about something which would happen in the future. One could almost say that he actualized what he proclaimed. When he announced that the kingdom of God was near at hand, he had in fact already brought it with him in such a way that its power could be experienced. The fact that evil spirits were compelled to surrender meant that the kingdom of God was making advances and that Satan was being driven back.

The same idea is made clear in the excitement of Jesus when his apostles reported how the unclean spirits were forced to obey their commands: "I saw Satan fall like lightning from heaven" (Luke 10:18). There is no real basis for having these words refer to an earlier visionary experience of Jesus. They are more naturally understood as a dramatic expression of the reaction of Jesus to the testimony of the apostles.

Taken by themselves, exorcisms probably have no special connection with any particular eschatological figure. We have already mentioned the possibility that the traditions concerning Solomon, the son of David, have colored messianic expectations. The most reasonable view is to understand the exorcisms as a clear sign of supernatural intervention, an expression that God is with the one who performs such mighty deeds (cf. Acts 10:38). But, of course, along with this there were tendencies in early Jewish eschatology to see reality in a cosmic, dualistic perspective as a struggle between the heavenly and demonic world of spirits.

From a historical perspective it is probably coincidental that exorcisms have come to be thought of as playing such an important role in Jesus' life and thought. Even though Luke 10:18, quoted above, is followed by a warning against rejoicing overly much over the subjection of the evil spirits, it appears as if Jesus himself considered it an essential part of his vocation to drive satanic forces out of the possessed and the sick. We should probably add that he regarded it as nothing less than a messianic task. The expulsion of evil spirits, therefore, becomes a clear sign of the breaking in of the kingdom of God.

"But I say. . ."

"And they were astonished at his teaching, for he taught them as one who had authority, and not as the scribes" (Mark 1:22). Formally, the way Jesus preached differed greatly from the sermons of the scribes. The difference is characterized quite strikingly with the reference to the "authority" of Jesus. The scribes routinely interpreted both Scripture and recognized authorities. Even the prophetic style, which was now known only from the Scriptures, contained a strong indication that prophets did not speak on their own behalf, but only reported what God had suggested to them and commanded them. But when Jesus preached, he did so with sovereign independence: "I say." Never did he use a circumlocution in the third person; for example, the expression "the Son of man says . . ." never occurs. While he used quotations from the Scripture, it does not appear that he ever preached on a particular text. Nor did he mention revelatory visions and auditions. He did not try to legitimate himself. When he began statements with "I say," it is not the divine "I" which used the prophet as a spokesperson. "I" means Jesus, yet what he announces is "the word of God." This obvious teaching authority, which Jesus felt no need to justify, is very striking, particularly in an early Jewish setting. Since it must be conceded that the preaching of John the Baptist had much the same character, it is possible that the conduct of Jesus in this matter was not completely without precedent and parallel. Yet the traditions of John the Baptist's preaching are altogether too fragmentary for drawing any significant conclusions.

The authority of Jesus is most astonishing when opposed to recognized teaching authorities. "You have heard that it was said to the men of old, but I say to you. . . . " This is the basic pattern of the antitheses in the first part of the Sermon on the Mount (Matt. 5:21-48). True enough, in particular instances it can be said that Jesus takes a stand on the side of the Law and simply validates its true intention (Matt. 5:21f.). In other instances, however, his teaching implies a basic criticism of the Law itself (Matt. 5:33-39). With regard to the question of divorce (Mark 10:2-9), the prescriptions of the Law get an apologetic interpretation. Yet they are nevertheless regarded as constituting an untenable departure from the clear will of God. The maxim which Jesus proposes in Mark 7:15—"There is nothing outside a man which by going into him can defile him"— undermines all of the verdicts of the Law about clean and unclean. The controversies about Sabbath observance arose partly because Jesus defended the freer practice found among ordinary people in Galilee against the rigorous regulations of the Pharisees. Yet it is also clear that Jesus in his interpretation and evaluation of the Sabbath command was in conflict with many passages in Scripture. It is not too surprising that he was accused of wanting to "abolish the law and the prophets" (Matt. 5:17).

What needs emphasis in this regard is the sovereign authority with which Jesus acted when he frequently, without any justification, and without appeal to tradition or the scribal authorities, presented his teaching as absolutely normative. We must observe that Jesus does this with the confident conviction that what he says represents the will of God, that it is true Torah. He does not comport himself as a sovereign lawgiver, who in his own authority decides what is right and proper. One must not presuppose a train of thought like the following: "That which Moses said to the people of old was adequate for that time, but I am greater than Moses and I say that from now on things shall be thus and so." His authority did not consist in the fact that he knew himself authorized to give out a new law. He did not act with royal prerogatives. It is probably not accidental that Jesus does not apply any particular title to himself in such contexts. That would have been inappropriate. Jesus did not give his Torah by virtue of the fact that he claimed a particular role or office. The evangelist Matthew, however, very possibly thought along those lines in presenting Jesus as the new Moses or the one who is greater than Moses. But it is exceedingly doubtful whether Jesus' authoritative "I" implied that he placed his own personal authority up against the authority of others.

We must be cautious in making the unqualified claim that it is specifically a *messianic* self-consciousness which Jesus reflects. It is more probable that he was so supremely confident that he was right, that the truth and propriety of what he taught was so self-evident for him, that any justification was really superfluous. In arguing in defense of his position or in trying to influence others, in several instances he appealed to common sense, to the universal sense of good and bad. Representative examples include the discussion about what is unclean in Mark 7 and the conflicts over Sabbath observance. Further specific examples of Jesus' arguments include: (1) The Sabbath was made for the sake of humans, not the reverse (Mark 2:27). (2) Should a person do good or evil on the Sabbath (Mark 3:4 and par.)? (3) Should not one who has been bound by Satan for many years be freed on the Sabbath (Luke 13:16)? So far it does not appear that Jesus promulgated a new teaching. He simply removed the scales from the eyes of people and disclosed the hypocrisy which had camouflaged the truth. With regard to his general instruction, therefore, there is no adequate reason to speak of an "interim ethic," a Torah for the short time remaining. What Jesus proclaimed was the eternal will of God, just as it was from the beginning (e.g., in the Sermon on the Mount). The situation is different when it comes to particular demands made on the disciples in particular situations. This subject will require further discussion below.

One formally distinct feature of Jesus' teaching is that he sometimes introduced sayings with "amen." Yet, no important conclusions can be drawn from that fact. We cannot assume that every saying introduced in that way is authentic, for such a striking stylistic peculiarity could easily be transferred and copied. Yet we must assume that some of these sayings are genuine. The significance of the introductory "amen" is to emphasize and call attention to what follows. The prefatory "amen" has a function analogous to such additions as "let the one who has ears to hear, listen." The message is important, but we cannot conclude anything about Jesus' view of himself on the basis of such features.

The Father and the Son

Many scholars place great emphasis on another distinctive emphasis of Jesus, his use of *abba* and particularly his way of speaking of God as Father.[16] Jesus approached God in prayer as *abba*, "Father," and when he spoke about God he often used the expressions "my Father," or "your Father," though "our Father" is not used. The phrase "Our Father," which introduces the Lord's Prayer in Matt. 6:9, is no exception, for it is a prayer intended for the *disciples*. The parallel in Luke 11:2 simply has "Father" (corresponding to *abba*). Though it is certain that the intimate term *abba* was characteristic of Jesus, it is difficult to decide how striking and uncommon it might have seemed at that time. With regard to the question of how he regarded himself, it is more important to learn whether his manner of speaking of God and to God as his own Father bears witness to the fact that he regarded God in a special and exclusive sense as his own Father. In other words, did Jesus consider himself to be God's "unique Son," "*the* Son"?

The evidence is not unambiguous. The translation of Jesus' words into Greek contributes to the uncertainty. It is striking that the Aramaic term *abba* was also used among Greek-speaking Christians (Rom. 8:15; Gal. 4:6). It appears that the use of *abba* as an address in prayer became a kind of distinguishing mark for Christians. But if it was a distinguishing feature which can be traced back to Jesus, it most obviously means that Jesus taught his disciples to say *abba* in the same way that he himself did, in other words, that he wanted them to look upon God as Father in the same way that he did. On the basis of the prayer formula *abba,* then, one cannot conclude that Jesus regarded himself as the Son of God in any unique sense.

There is a great deal of evidence indicating that there is no obstacle in joining an exclusive conception of "the Son" with a comprehensive conception of a group in which all are sons of God or children of God, whether the latter is thought to be based on a derivative relationship or not. By *derivative* we mean that because Jesus is the Son of God in the primary sense, those who belong to him are also able to call themselves children of God. The Gospel of John is pervaded with the interplay between "the Father" and "the Son." The problem is whether this symbolism actually has a historical basis in the fact that Jesus himself expressed the view that he was the Son of God in a special sense.

The so-called prayer of thanksgiving in Matt. 11:25-27 = Luke 10:21-24 presents us with an unsolved problem of tradition criticism and historical criticism. According to form and content this pericope appears more suitable for the Gospel of John than for the synoptic Gospels. It is possible that we are brought a step closer to a solution thanks to the Qumran texts, since it appears that the distinctive features of Johannine thought and expression may be due to an Essene element in the Christian community. The prayer of thanksgiving calls to mind some of the psalms of praise we know from Qumran. The distinctive self-consciousness reflected in these psalms points to the teacher of righteousness as their author. He knew that he had been chosen by God and that he, through the Spirit, had received insight into the mysteries of God. The strong emphasis on the fact that everything is sovereignly predetermined by God is also present (cf. 1QH 2:10,13,18,32; 3:21f.; 4:5, 27). But the father/son motif is lacking in Qumran, as well as the negative application of "those who are wise and understanding" (Matt. 11:25; Luke 10:21). That God has concealed "these things" from the learned and revealed them to the ignorant is a motif which harmonizes well with Jesus' attitude as reflected in the synoptic Gospels. There a prominent feature is that the gospel is proclaimed to the poor, that the sick need a physician, that tax collectors and prostitutes precede

Pharisees and scribes. But for the most part this pericope is so atypical of the proclamation of Jesus in both form and content—and in addition so Johannine—that we are compelled to disregard it.

Mark 13:32 must also be judged inauthentic: "But of that day or that hour no one knows, not even the angels in heaven, nor the Son, but only the Father." Some scholars have contended that such a saying cannot have originated with the Christian community, because they regarded Jesus as omniscient. Yet, that argument can be turned around: here it is presupposed that Jesus as the Son of God knows more than the angels. Such a way of thinking does not cohere well with the portrait of Jesus in the synoptic Gospels, apart from such apocalyptic texts as Mark 13. It is precisely texts of this type which, from the perspective of tradition criticism, have a weak claim to authenticity.

In this connection it is appropriate to consider the parable of the wicked tenants (Mark 12:1-12; Luke 20:9-19; Matt. 21:33-46; Gospel of Thomas 65–66). It is easy to understand how this parable has been understood as an allegory. The disloyal tenants are Israel's leaders, the servants stand for the prophets, and the son is Jesus. Many have regarded this as an allegory which originated with the Christian community. But in the Gospel of Thomas the patently allegorical elements are missing. C. H. Dodd,[17] later supported by Joachim Jeremias,[18] argued convincingly that the original story was a pure parable in typical form. It contained three examples with the emphasis on the last (the folkloristic principles of sets of three and of final emphasis) and with actual relevance to the historical situation in Palestine at the time of Jesus. The owner of the vineyard, who lived in the diaspora, first sent two servants, one after the other, to collect the profits. They were brutally turned away (with no mention of anyone being killed). The owner finally sent his son, confident that they would not dare resist him. But the tenants had no scruples. They thought that he must be the heir come to take over the vineyard, and that if they eliminated him, they themselves could become the owners. But they made a fatal miscalculation. There is nothing artificial about the story. Yet there can be no doubt about the application: it is aimed at Jesus' opponents in the Sanhedrin, and even the allegorical version preserves the correct interpretation.

An important question is whether in the parable Jesus indirectly calls himself the Son of God and places himself in a very special

relationship to God. It is easy to answer yes. But the fact is that
"the only son" is an essential feature of the parable itself, for otherwise the disloyal tenants' way of thinking and acting would have
no basis. The concept "son" is therefore indispensable for the re-
alism of the story itself, though not for its application. It can be
applied to Jesus without the necessity of considering Jesus as the
Son of God. It is sufficient that he plays a different and more decisive
role than the servants. That is true, at any rate, if Jesus is the
Messiah. For the Messiah is unique, the last, and the heir to the
throne. For that matter, he can also be called the Son of God (Ps.
2:7; 2 Sam. 7:12-14). The opponents of Jesus could hardly hear the
parable and understand its point without drawing the conclusion that
Jesus identified himself with the Messiah. And they could also easily
infer that he had called himself "Son of God."

It does not appear incredible that Jesus would have provoked
his opponents with such a parable on one of the final days of his
life. It is no easier to believe that it was placed in his mouth by the
Christian community, since it lacks any reference to Jesus' resurrection. The parable is, to be sure (also in the Gospel of Thomas)
followed by a quotation from Scripture about the stone which was
rejected by the builders but which ended up as the cornerstone. Yet
this is a very different use of metaphor, so that the combination can
be secondary and occasioned by the need for something which could
point toward the resurrection. The application of Scripture is typically Christian. The parable probably originated with Jesus in a form
not very much different from that in Luke 20:9-16. It reflects a
messianic consciousness, but does not indicate that Jesus is the Son
of God in any other sense than can be claimed for the Messiah.

David's Lord

A remarkable pericope is placed in the context of Jesus' activity
in Jerusalem. The Markan version forms part of Jesus teaching in
the temple (12:35-37), but the parallels in Matt. 22:41-46 and Luke
12:41-44 conclude a series of conflict stories involving scribes. They
were also targets of Jesus, according to Mark 12:35. While it is
characteristic of conflict stories that it is the opponents who try to
corner Jesus, here it is Jesus who takes the offensive and asks them
a question which they are unable to answer. When David himself
in Psalm 110:1 calls the Messiah "Lord," how then can the Messiah

be David's son? For the evangelists the answer must have been obvious, for they left the question both unanswered and unexplained. For modern scholars, however, the question has certainly proved as perplexing as it was for those ancient scribes.

If the situation had been that the scribes argued against connecting messianic expectations with Jesus by showing that the Messiah had to be a descendant of David (and Jesus was not), then this way of posing the problem would become comprehensible, at least as an expression of Christian apologetics. The Epistle of Barnabas 12:10 contains a polemic against calling Jesus David's son since he is God's Son; the title "Son of man" is also rejected. It is certainly conceivable that Jesus did not consider himself as belonging to the house of David and that he made no such claim. Yet, for the evangelists the tradition of his descent from David was an absolute and unassailable fact and therefore of Christological significance. Their solution cannot be reconciled with that of the Epistle of Barnabas. They had to presuppose an answer which granted that the Messiah was David's son, but which also held that he was God's Son, and is properly designated David's *Lord*. But in which trap are the scribes caught?

The point could well be analogous with that which we considered in the problem of authority in Mark 11:27-33, that is, that the scribes are cornered, not because they are without understanding, but because the answer will be used against them. Here is an example of a response which might have proven problematic for the scribes: David can call the Messiah "Lord," even if he is his son—because he also is God's Son. That appears plausible if their complaint against Jesus was not that he wanted to be the Messiah, but that he intimated that he was God's Son. And that is not impossible; the parable of the wicked tenants is just one among several possible sources for that idea. It was on just such a basis that Jesus was ultimately condemned for blasphemy. That one man was held by some to be the coming Messiah and that he perhaps thought so himself was no real basis for attacking him. The situation would be different, however, if it could be charged that he blasphemously claimed to be God's Son. In such circumstances it would be a disarming answer to show that according to the Scriptures the Messiah was more than simply the son of David. But would it not have been easier to point directly to those texts which call the Messiah the Son of God?

We have found a possible opening for situating this pericope into a context which fits into the history of Jesus. But that does not mean that we can be certain of dealing with a piece of authentic tradition. No text was exploited more industriously in the Christological argumentation of the early church than Psalm 110. It would have been tempting to have Jesus himself use it against the skeptical Jews. In Heb. 1:3, 13; 8:1; 10:12), Psalm 110 is used partly for demonstrating the superiority of Jesus to angels, and partly for proving that he is the priest of an order higher than that of the Jewish high priests. A closer analogy to the use of Psalm 110 in Mark 12 can be found in Acts 2:34-35, for here it is David himself to whom it is compared. In the context (vv. 25-28), Ps. 16:8-11 is used in a similar manner. These psalms speak of one who was not delivered over to death, but took his seat beside God, while David is dead and buried without anyone ever suggesting that he had ascended to heaven. David was therefore speaking in the Spirit about the Messiah, that is, Jesus. Mark 12:35-37 becomes comprehensible within a Christian apologetic biblical exegesis of this type. Since we find ourselves at a point within the gospel narrative preceding Jesus' death and resurrection, it is readily comprehensible that the question remains unanswered, as an enigmatic suggestion of a mystery. That corresponds to the evangelist's idea of the messianic secret, which cannot be disclosed or comprehended before Jesus has risen from the dead. If there is relatively great probability that the words are secondary, it serves no good purpose to speculate further about what they could have meant had they been authentic.

"For my sake"

There are various sayings of Jesus which ascribe a decisive significance to the relationship which people had to Jesus himself. The evidence is not homogeneous. It naturally includes more sayings than those which contain the formula "for my sake," but we can begin with them.[19] Many of these sayings seem to reflect the situation of the later Christian community. For example, persecution for the sake of Jesus was a common phenomenon. In some cases the phrase "for my sake" may be a secondary addition. It is unnecessary to discuss all instances, but we should mention a few which are very likely authentic. Mark 10:29 and Matt. 19:29 contain a promise for all who have forsaken home, family, and possessions for the sake of Jesus. That corresponds to the demand to follow Jesus which finds an appropriate setting in the life of Jesus. But the parallel in Luke 18:29 reads "for the sake of the kingdom of God," which could equally well be authentic. Yet, on the other hand, Luke 22:28-30 contains a saying with a related point, to the effect that those who have shared Jesus' testings are promised places of honor in the messianic kingdom. In both Matt. 5:11 and Luke 6:22, the series of beatitudes ends with rejoicing over those who are scorned and persecuted for the sake of Jesus. The wording can reflect the situation of the later Christian community, but in and of itself there is nothing to forbid us from taking such a saying as this as authentic. It is historically probable that the followers of Jesus experienced scorn and derision. Yet the phrase "for my [or, 'the Son of man's'] sake" could well be an interpolation. It is in any case questionable how personally the possibly genuine phrase "for my sake" must be understood, whether it connotes "for the sake of my cause," or "because you have listened to me." It is not advisable to base too much on this material.

If we now go on to examine other sayings which link people's fate to their positive or negative response to Jesus, we must attempt to differentiate those sayings which actually deal with support for the person of Jesus and those which involve hearing and obeying his word. For example, in the parable of the house builders which concludes the Sermon on the Mount (Matt. 7:24-27 = Luke 6:47-49), salvation and condemnation are linked to whether a person will live in accordance with the program Jesus has proclaimed, not particularly because it is *his* message, but because the Sermon on the Mount interprets God's eternal love. The story contains, to be sure, a section which includes the person of Jesus (7:21-22), but aside from the fact that this element is hardly authentic, it nevertheless underscores the fact that the decisive thing is not calling Jesus Lord, but performing the will of God.[20]

The parable of the sower in Mark 4 and par. should not be given that title, since the one who broadcasts the seed is irrelevant for understanding the point of the parable. According to the explanation appended to the parable, it concerns those who hear the word of God but respond to it in different ways. Originally this parable probably concerned the kingdom of God and was related to the parables of growth, which optimistically maintain that even if things sometimes look impossible and everything goes wrong, all reverses will be forgotten when the kingdom is present in all its glory.[21]

Among the sayings which unambiguously make decisive the relation to the person of Jesus, Luke 12:8f. is probably the most significant:[22]

> Every one who acknowledges me before men, the Son of man also will acknowledge before the angels of God; but he who denies me before men will be denied before the angels of God.

Rudolf Bultmann and many others think that this saying is probably authentic because it clearly indicates that, when Jesus (in authentic sayings) speaks of the Son of man, he did not think of himself, but of the apocalyptic savior figure who would be revealed to execute the final judgment of God.[23] The meaning must therefore be that the Son of man will come to pronounce judgment on the basis of the faithfulness or faithlessness of individuals toward Jesus. Of course, none of the evangelists would have agreed that the saying should be understood in that manner. That Jesus was the Son of man was so obvious that it did not occur to any of the evangelists to guard themselves against the misunderstanding that the Son of man might be someone else. The interchangeability of the first person pronoun *I* or *me* with the phrase "Son of man" has been readily explained in this century (after the notion of an apocalyptic Son of man was commonly accepted by exegetes) with the proposal that *Son of man* was the title which complemented Jesus' eschatological function as judge. For those (like the present author) who consider the entire theory of an apocalyptic "Son of man" title as mistaken, it is more appropriate to explain the interchange on a purely stylistic basis. It is a basic poetic device in Semitic poetry to interchange synonymous terms in parallel lines. Thereby a cumulative effect is achieved in specific instances in which the synonyms "man" and "son of man" are used in a poetic couplet. The real meaning is that Jesus as the Son of man will testify before the heavenly throne of judgment, supporting those who faithfully stood by his side, but dissociating himself from those who did not wish to acknowledge him. While the Son of man in the parallel texts, Mark 8:38 and Luke 9:26, acts as a judge, here in Luke 12:8f. (as in Rev. 3:5), he is more appropriately regarded as the crucial witness before God's throne of judgment. The apocalyptic motif of the parousia is not in view.

In spite of the strong attestation and the Semitic tone, one cannot say that the saying belongs to those logia which have an indisputable claim to be considered genuine. As a saying of Jesus it must have been directed to the disciples and understood as an appeal to remain steadfast by his side regardless of the cost. Formally it is related to the sayings about discipleship.

"If any one would come after me, let him deny himself and take up his cross and follow me. For whoever would save his life will lose it; and whoever loses his life for my sake will save it" (Mark 8:34-35; Matt. 16:24-25; Luke 9:23-24; cf. Matt. 10:37-39 and Luke 14:26-27). There is some variation in wording, but the point is generally clear: the one who will follow Jesus must abandon everything else, give up all personal interests, and make common cause with Jesus. That could cost a person his life, but if one lays down his life for the sake of Jesus, he has really saved it. On the other hand, if he should attempt to save himself, he will really forfeit his life. While Matthew emphasizes the relevance of the saying for the disciples, it appears that Mark, and Luke even more clearly, gives it a general validity, regardless of the fact that the historical situation had changed. The general conditions for being accepted as a Christian are formulated in this total demand for self-denial for the sake of Jesus. In the life and proclamation of the church, there is no difference between the phrases "for Jesus' sake" and "for the sake of (the kingdom of) God."

If we inquire about the historical situation and the significance which these words must originally have had, the phrase "for Jesus' sake" can only be considered authentic if directed to the little flock who literally followed Jesus. They then correspond to the sayings on discipleship in Luke 9:57-62 and Matt. 8:19-22, and the promises to those who have forsaken all (Mark 10:28-30; Matt. 19:27-29; Luke 18:20-30; cf. Luke 22:28-30). It was not the duty of everyone to follow Jesus. For one thing, not every one was free to join himself to the company of Jesus; it was an honor and a task for which one must be granted permission. For another thing, a very different set of demands regarding actual self-denial was placed on those who followed him and made common cause with him than was placed on ordinary followers. The former shared Jesus' lot because they shared his calling. That is, Jesus appears very much like countless revolutionary leaders throughout history. Naturally there are different types of leaders of popular movements. Some have devoted themselves to a sacred calling, while others struggle to attain personal objectives, for example, to win the throne to which they think themselves entitled. "For my sake" need not mean that Jesus' own status is involved, as though the disciples were those chosen to fight to make him Messiah. The point can just as well be that the conspirators submitted to a natural leader in order to devote themselves to the fight for the cause he has convinced them to believe in. Whether it is said "for my name's sake" (Matt. 19:29), "for my sake and for the gospel" (Mark 10:29), or "for the sake of the kingdom of God" (Luke 18:29), it need not make any material difference. Because Jesus completely identified himself with the gospel and the concerns of the kingdom of God, it must have been very natural for both him and his disciples to equate a yes or no to him with a yes or no to God. At any rate it is incorrect to claim that the salvation and condemnation mentioned in such sayings is made dependent on the position one takes to Jesus. He does not stand out here as the savior of either the people or individuals. The possibility is definitely present that Jesus could place such total demands on his disciples and at the same time recognize John the Baptist and his followers—and possibly other such dedicated groups—as equally good and worthy children of God.

At this point perhaps it is appropriate to say a few words about the judgment scene depicted in Matt. 25:31-46. This passage is commonly called a *parable* about the last judgment. Yet the only feature reminiscent of a parable is the interpolated comparison of the judgment scene with a shepherd's task of separating the sheep from the goats (vv. 32-33). Apart from that we have a stylized, dramatic description of the day of judgment. The basis for judgment is what people have done or left undone for the Son of man, not directly, but indirectly through their relationship to "the least of his brethren." The passage can be interpreted in two different ways, either that the basis for judgment is simply whether one has acted humanely because the Son of man represents every person who needs compassion and help, or that the criterion is the relationship to the Son of man's "least brethren" in the sense of Jesus' disciples (cf. Matt. 10:42). Only in this latter instance could it be said that the criterion for judgment was the relationship to the person of Jesus, since one could claim that people's treatment of the followers of Jesus was an expression of their love or hate toward Jesus himself. Any interpretation along these lines ought to require a much clearer pointer than that indicated by the expression "the least of my brethren." With the other interpretation the text suggests a popular motif in folklore: the king who finds out for himself what people really are like by going around in disguise. The passage under consideration presupposes the notion of the return of Jesus as judge, but there are features which suggest that the introduction (vv. 31-33) is secondary (note how the Son of man in v. 31 is replaced by the king in v. 34). If we begin with v. 34, there is the strong possibility that the king in a more original version represented God. The moral of the story would then really be the simple, fundamental principle that no one loves God if he hates his neighbor. That would harmonize well with the teachings of Jesus. The version in Matthew 25 is, at any rate, secondary.

Our preliminary conclusion, based on this overview of the indirect self-testimony of the traditional words of Jesus, must be that it is doubtful that there is any authentic tradition which makes the person of Jesus central, to the extent that it is *he* who acts as savior or judge, and it is *he* upon whom people's fate depends. That which determines salvation or condemnation is whether one receives the message of the kingdom of God and becomes obedient to the will of God, not whether one associates with the man Jesus. Jesus projects an almost boundless confidence that his understanding of the will of God is correct; thus his words take on an unconditional authority, but invoke for himself no special position or authorization and certainly no messianic title. That clearly implies a consciousness of being called and sent by God, and this prophetic consciousness— if one can call it that—gets its distinctive character through the eschatological perspective, which makes him the last and therefore most crucial proclaimer of the message of salvation. But that his own person is part of the message, we dare not maintain. He proclaims the Father, not the Son. It is Jesus' word, not his person, which will never pass away (for that matter, it is doubtful whether Matt. 24:35 is a genuine saying of Jesus, even if it is essentially similar to the assurance of a prophetic calling).

When it concerns the obvious authority which characterizes his proclamation and teaching, we may harbor the reservation that the picture is stamped by the church's conception of Jesus Christ. It is not certain that what Jesus ought to say was so simple and clear for him. In fact, the tradition contains certain features which can indicate that he could be in doubt and perplexity, certainly not about the general will of God, but at least about the relation of God's will to himself. In the symbolic story of the temptation in the wilderness he certainly acts in a sovereign manner; but the sharp words to Peter—that he was an offense to him, tempting him to evade his destiny—indicate that Jesus had to struggle with himself, as the Gethsemane tradition also attests. When it is reported several times that he spent a long time in solitary prayer, particularly before important decisions (Mark 1:35; 6:46; Luke 6:12; 9:18,28), it is obvious that even the evangelists thought that he must seek strength and guidance. The portrait of a man who always without further ado knew what he must say and do does not thoroughly correspond with the thrust of the gospel traditions (cf. also Heb. 5:7).

8

The Testimony of Jesus' Deeds

The gospel proclaimed by early Christians pointed to Jesus' deeds as proof that God was with him. At that time it was primarily his miracles which were in view. We will expand the scope much further. The question for us is whether his actions and his manner of life reveal anything about how he regarded himself and how he interpreted his role. We assume that his activities reflect a conscious program, and that his behavior often had symbolic significance. When we examine his deeds in the light of his message and interpret his sayings in the context of his actions, possibilities are opened for achieving a comprehensive perspective which can provide a specific answer to the question of who he considered himself to be. The deeds in isolation do not provide a clear answer. But it must be granted that it is difficult to interpret the "statement" made through his deeds even if we pay attention to their context. In addition, there is even greater uncertainty regarding the historical trustworthiness of the traditions of Jesus' conduct than with the transmission of Jesus' proclamation.

The Miracles

The "mighty deeds" Jesus performed are both regarded and reiterated in the tradition as miracles of *legitimation*. One of the features which suggests the trustworthiness of several of the miracle stories is the fact that they do *not* give the impression that the motif of legitimation was essential for Jesus. Most of his miracles are not primarily demonstrations of power, but acts of mercy originating in a spontaneous compassion for people who are suffering. Jesus was primarily concerned with healing of the sick and the possessed.

A historian finds difficulties with the entire body of evidence, and is compelled to brand a large part of it as legendary. In this group is included the nature miracles, even though it is possible that they have a historical core. With regard to the miracle of the loaves, it does not help to argue that it was performed out of compassion, for in this case even the need is legendary! With the miracles of healing the situation is quite different, primarily in the case of exorcisms. There can be no doubt about the fact that Jesus in many instances restored sick and possessed people to health. Demon possession was a common diagnosis at that time, and could include a variety of diseases and mental disturbances. In particular cases such a detailed description of symptoms is provided that a specific medical diagnosis can be proposed. Mark 9:14-27, for example, describes epilepsy. As a matter of fact, Jesus not only performed healings and exorcisms, but also thought himself in possession of power to perform miracles.

With respect to the extent of this activity, the notice that he could not perform more than a very few mighty deeds in his hometown because of the unbelief of the populace (Matt. 13:58; Mark 6:5-6) is both interesting and illuminating. The point of this episode for the evangelists was the censure of Jesus' hometown for its unbelief. Yet, the story reveals that the number of actual miracles was sharply limited, making it reasonable to conclude that Jesus often tried to perform healings without much success. Presumably, he found an explanation in people's lack of faith. *Faith* here primarily means confidence in God but also trust in the authority of Jesus to act on behalf of God or, expressed more popularly, belief in his supernatural powers. Faith should not be understood in terms of its meaning in late Christian theology. Other references to the fact that Jesus healed "all," or "a crowd," are generalizing exaggerations.

We can, it is true, conclude from an authentic saying of Jesus, namely, his cry of woe over Chorazin, Bethsaida, and Capernaum (Matt. 11:20-24 = Luke 10:12-15), that miracles of healing took place which were not described in the Gospels. But the frequently detailed individual accounts, which constitute a great part of the tradition, also indirectly attest to the fact that there were relatively few actual instances of miraculous healing, at any rate when compared with the great number of sick and disabled among the people. We have no idea of how frequently Jesus tried in vain to help the needy; the narrative is silent on such matters.

On the basis of many analogies we know that people with "supernatural faculties" do not lose their self-confidence even though their failures might outnumber their successes. Jesus offered several possibilities to explain why he was able to help only a few, and lack of faith was just one of them. In Luke 4:16-30, a relatively independent parallel to the report of the unbelief in Jesus' hometown, the response of Jesus is suggested in his reference to the fact that there were many lepers in Israel in the time of Elisha, but the only one the prophet was commissioned to cleanse was a Syrian. In the same way Elijah was sent to a poor widow in Zarephath in the land of Sidon, though there were many who were desperately ill in Israel. God is sovereign and bestows his gift upon whomever he will, and those who imagine that they have some right to be helped must often learn a hard lesson. Nazareth did not occupy a privileged position even though Jesus originated there, just as Israel did not own God despite the fact that they were very definitely God's elect people. Other explanations could be based on dualistic conceptions of human beings as fields of battle, or as plunder for contending forces. Satan must be conquered before all his victims can be liberated. That Jesus in the name of God managed to expel demons from possessed individuals attested to the fact that the kingdom of God was about to break in. Yet his exorcisms were only a foretaste of the complete liberation when the kingdom had come "with power" (Mark 9:1).

For Jesus, miracles were closely linked to the proclamation of the imminent kingdom of God. They were signs of the kingdom's inbreaking, warnings of the fact that the prince of demons had at last met his match. Whether the miracles were performed by Jesus himself or by his disciples in his name, they testified to the fact that the time of salvation was near. The powers of the coming kingdom were already at work. The miracles were not "messianic" signs in the sense that they provided concrete legitimation for Jesus as Messiah. Jesus, according to strongly attested tradition, considered the demand for miraculous proof to be an expression of sinful unbelief (Mark 8:11-13; Matt. 12:38f.; 16:1-4; Luke 11:16, 29; John 6:30; cf. Matt. 4:1-11 = Luke 4:1-13; 1 Cor. 1:22). Moreover, as observable signs miracles are always ambiguous (cf. the widespread conceptions of the miracles performed by the Antichrist, which, of course, assume a firm expectation that the Messiah would perform miracles).

It is remarkable that Jesus to all appearances regarded it as part of his mission to raise up the sick and liberate the possessed (cf. Luke 13:32), even though that was something no one expected of the Messiah or which was not even a necessary feature of the image of a prophet. In this respect there must have been a characteristic difference between John and Jesus, for there is no trace of a miracle tradition associated with John the Baptist (there are not even any hints that some of the miracles told of Jesus had been transferred to him from John). That it was only Jesus (and his disciples) who performed miracles must have been one of the most striking features which separated the two revival movements from each other and gave an air of distinction to each of them. The miracles belonged with the message of joy, not with prophecies of judgment.

Belief in miracles and the assurance of having divine authority for commanding the unclean spirits to abandon their victims belongs to those historical and cultural conditioning factors which magnify the obstacles that prevent an insight into Jesus' inner life. The most difficult point is to determine the influence of miracles and belief in miracles on his self-understanding and his personal vision of the future. If he regarded himself as the one chosen to become the Messiah, and at the same time thought it part of his calling to perform mighty deeds, we must also reckon with the possibility that he anticipated that miracles could happen in his own life. Some of those who sought refuge in the temple during the final phase of the siege of Jerusalem in A.D. 70, despite the fact that every human hope for salvation for the starving and demoralized defenders appeared to have vanished long before, still clung desperately to the promise that God would intervene when the situation appeared darkest and liberate the holy place and restore his kingdom. Cannot the description of Jesus' final hours narrated in Mark 15 be read in a similar way? Could not Jesus have held out the hope to the last cry of desperation that a miracle would happen? That is a possibility difficult to ignore, once it has been seriously considered. Yet that was certainly not what the evangelist intended when he allowed Jesus' last utterance to be the cry of dereliction from Psalm 22, "My God, my God, why hast thou forsaken me?" (Mark 15:34 and par.). On the whole, the sources provide an excellent basis for suspecting that Jesus seriously reckoned with the necessity of dying, but that he also looked forward to a miraculous resurrection.

Disciples and apostles

One of the features more difficult to interpret is the tradition that Jesus selected 12 men who followed him on his wanderings, were instructed by him, and were entrusted with tasks as his emissaries. There must be a historical basis for these traditions. The phrase "the Twelve" already occurs as a concept in the tradition referred to by Paul in 1 Cor. 15:5. The story that one of the Twelve betrayed Jesus can hardly be regarded as a later invention. In my opinion, it is also probable that the designation *apostle*, with the meaning "emissary," goes back to Jesus himself. At the very least, it was in use within the circle of his disciples during his lifetime.

The real issue is how the selection of 12 disciples and the sending out of the apostles should be interpreted. Is there any connection with Jesus' own selection as Messiah? Is the number *twelve* a symbol based on the tradition of the 12 tribes of Israel and the expectation of an eschatological regathering of the dispersed tribes? Luke 22:30 and Matt. 19:28 reproduce different versions of a prophetic promise by Jesus that the 12 disciples will one day sit, each on his own throne, as his official vicegerents judging the 12 tribes of Israel. This saying is possibly authentic, because it is difficult to understand how else it could have originated. It has only weak ties to Jewish conceptions, where one could certainly dream of a resurrection and reinstallation of the 12 patriarchs as tribal chiefs, but the leadership of men with no connection to each particular tribe is scarcely conceivable. In the early church there is no trace of a conception that the college of apostles regarded themselves as called to any such task. Moreover, the unfortunate story of Judas would have made it difficult to attribute such a saying to Jesus. There is certainly no necessity for understanding the saying in such a way that each of the Twelve will rule over his own tribe. They can be thought of as associate judges when he as Messiah will sit in judgment of Israel. In any case the point is a promise that they who had shared Jesus' lot and troubles in this life would receive their reward in the future kingdom (cf. Luke 22:28). There is a serious objection against crediting Jesus with sayings of this kind, however, since they do not fit with the impression that he never—not even within the circle of his disciples—openly proclaimed himself as Messiah. We dare not base too much on this saying in connection with Jesus' testimony about himself. Neither can we use it to establish the symbolic meaning of the number *twelve*. It is quite possible that the symbolism was included later, and that the number *twelve* was originally only a round number (e.g., "a dozen"), and it cannot be ruled out that it was simply a coincidence which led to the fact that Jesus' steadfast followers were arbitrarily constituted by 12 (rather than 11 or 13) men. Nor are we any the wiser for drawing upon the Qumran community for comparison. They had a council of 12 laymen and 3 priests (1QS 8–9). The 12 probably represent "Israel" and the 3 "Aaron" (cf. the 3 priestly clans mentioned in Num. 3:17—Gershon, Kohath, and Merari). Otherwise the number *twelve* plays no important role at Qumran.

There are indications which suggest that only during the lifetime of Jesus were "the Twelve" a clearly defined group of disciples. The group later lost its significance. There has never even been conclusive evidence for all their names. Acts 1:15-25, to be sure, describes the selection of a replacement for Judas (even here there is no evidence for the symbolic significance of the number *twelve*). But what really happened was that men outside this circle began to play a much more important role than some of the Twelve. Most prominent among those who were originally outsiders was James the brother of Jesus, though Barnabas was also significant, not to mention Paul.

It is far from certain whether Jesus ascribed symbolic significance to the number *twelve* as representing the tribes of Israel or the core of a new Israel. But what was his intention in selecting these men? What role was intended for them? Jesus demanded that they forsake everything to follow him. They were to free themselves from all social ties, relinquish all economic security, follow him through thick and thin, and be prepared to sacrifice their lives. These are the kinds of requirements which a person like Judas Maccabeus might have demanded of his men. Yet the analogy breaks down, since Jesus was certainly no Zealot revolutionary or guerrilla leader. It is just the total demands, the unshakable solidarity, and the obvious obedience to the leader that are reminiscent of revolutionary military groups. In other respects the group of disciples had less in common with a guerrilla unit than the Salvation Army has with the armed forces of a modern nation. On the other hand, we could begin with the term *disciple* and find an analogy with the scribes and their schools. Yet it is obvious that the similarities are superficial, since no rabbi would ever prescribe such requirements. In ancient days there were prophetic guilds which might have provided a pattern (Isa. 8:16-18); compare the story of how Elijah called Elisha to be his disciple (1 Kings 19:19-21; cf. Luke 9:59f.). The Qumran community offers some points of similarity, even if their monastic life had little in common with the itinerant existence of the disciples. Particularly relevant are the rigorous demands placed on novices, including instruction and a probationary period. John the Baptist also had disciples, though we know very little about how they were organized. Yet it is probable that there were many points of similarity. Common to all such groups (with the exception of guerrilla bands) is their religious character and the close relationship between teacher and pupils.

But to what end did the disciples of Jesus require training? What was the goal of their education? What were they expected to become? What is the connection between the calling of Jesus and the calling of his disciples? Obviously the answer must lie in the fact that the disciples were trained either to provide support for Jesus in his own task or to carry on his work after his death. Actually, both objectives could have been pursued simultaneously. The tradition of the calling of the disciples (Mark 3:13-19; Luke 6:12-19) reflects the first objective: their selection is a preparation for the sending out of the apostles (Mark 6:7-11; Luke 9:1-5; cf. Matt. 10:1-16). The content of the instruction given to the disciples, on the other hand, is dominated by concerns for the future following Jesus' death. Since this motif is already evident in the speeches in which he commissions the disciples, it is easy to suppose that a shift may have occurred in the tradition. It is uncertain whether Jesus' teaching was really focused on the future to the extent suggested in the Gospels. This problem is inseparable from the whole question of Jesus' conceptions of the future.

In addition to the sending out of the Twelve, Luke tells about the 72 who were sent out on a later occasion, though the latter narrative is doubtless due to Luke's familiarity with two versions, in one of which the number *72* (a number also based on biblical models and perhaps freighted with symbolic meaning), has replaced the number *12* that occurs in the other. The textual variants vacillate between 70 and 72, probably due to the fact that both numbers occur in other connections, e.g., the 70 elders in ancient Israel and in the later Sanhedrin, and the 72 or 70 nations of the world. Both numbers have a certain magical value, 7 x 10 and 6 x 12. The text suggests no particular symbolic significance. Both variants appear equally well attested and equally appropriate. The historical issue is whether Jesus ever on any occasion sent out disciples in pairs on a special mission. It cannot be disputed that within the scope of Jesus' activity the sending out of the disciples stands out as a remarkably disjunctive episode. Basically it has no consequences, no continuation, and only Luke 10:17f. makes a point out of what the apostles had experienced.[24]

It is not easy to take a confident position on the problem of historicity. If everything found in the account of the sending out of the Twelve were removed from the Gospels, no one would have missed it. On the other hand, it seems ill advised to imagine a kind of retrojection of later ecclesiastical missionary practice or missionary instruction, since what is known of the oldest missionary activity does not provide an appropriately corresponding picture. If we suspect that the sending out of the Twelve occurred, we still have a difficult time grasping its significance. That is particularly the case when we attempt to understand it on the basis of the messianic consciousness of Jesus. It seems more appropriate to understand the situation on the basis of the eschatological prophet's conviction that the kingdom of God is in the process of breaking in, which involves carrying the joyful message to people as quickly as possible. That would happen too slowly if Jesus alone were saddled with that task. Therefore he delegated others, whom he had instructed, and gave them authority both to preach and to expel evil spirits. One can then vividly imagine that the sending out of the Twelve concluded with the observation that they would not have finished visiting the cities of Israel before the kingdom of God had come (cf. Matt. 10:23; Mark 9:1). But, in fact, it looked as if the whole project had come to nothing. The apostles returned to Jesus and everything was as before. Is the explanation that things did not go as Jesus had expected? Did he have to revise his eschatological expectations? Did the instruction of the disciples then begin to take on a new character so that it became preparation for a more distant future? It is, at any rate, obvious that the speech connected with the sending out of the Twelve was revised in Matthew 10 and has been expanded in a way appropriate for the later ecclesiastical situation of persecution.

From the perspective of the evangelists, the sending out of delegated disciples as Jesus' apostles almost appears to be a practical exercise with the view to a future missionary activity. As a link in Jesus' activity it can only be understood as a way of making sure that the message of the kingdom of God was effectively proclaimed so that all Jews would have a chance to be converted and believe the gospel. To that extent it simply means that Jesus permitted an extension of his own calling, utilizing the most steadfast of his followers and fellow workers. The instruction to go without taking along any type of equipment of the sort necessary for travelers can be interpreted in several ways. Primarily it should be taken as an indication of urgency, but also as a symbolic expression of liberation from all this-worldly security and unconditional trust in God's care for his own. In this way it is possible to understand the call of the disciples and their sending out in agreement with Jesus' prophetic, premessianic task as his own forerunner. There is no convincing way of explaining that the sending out of the Twelve stands out as an isolated interlude. It appears to have been limited to Galilee and must have been concluded before the journey to Jerusalem could begin (cf. Mark 1:38). From such a perspective Luke 10:17-20 could make sense (if it is connected to Luke 9:10). The mission is carried out to the joy of the disciples and the satisfaction of Jesus.

In the structure of Mark, the episode at Caesarea Philippi focused on Peter's confession, and was the turning point for Jesus and his followers. The instruction of the disciples received a very different emphasis and the calling of the disciples a new dimension. The Twelve are those who would go with Jesus to Jerusalem and who would be initiated into the messianic mystery, so that they could later interpret and proclaim the meaning of the cross. Even if we are dealing with a reconstruction based on a later ecclesiastical perspective, it is not without some basis in fact. But we cannot go any further. The selection of the Twelve and what is narrated about them does not really help us a great deal in understanding the nature of Jesus' messianic consciousness, even if we are dealing with a distinctive phenomenon.

The invitation to "tax collectors and sinners"

All versions of the life of Jesus place great emphasis on the fact that Jesus associated with people who were not welcome in polite society, and that he "ate with tax collectors and sinners." That was the kind of behavior which the Pharisees and other upright people found thoroughly offensive. Here we undoubtedly have another important factor which sheds light on Jesus' self-understanding. Yet we should not ignore the sociological and psychological perspective which suggests that we be somewhat wary of overemphasizing the sensational aspects of Jesus' relationship to the dispossessed. Jesus grew up in an insignificant little village with a homogeneous Jewish population and a single synagogue. No rich people lived in Nazareth, there were no tax collectors, and it is doubtful if there was any excessive poverty. When a marriage was celebrated or a funeral mourned in a family, the whole village probably took part. The Pharisees (and the Essenes) attempted to separate themselves from the ignorant masses who were unfamiliar with the Law. They distanced themselves from the social structure of the villages. Yet the conditions in small villages would never allow this to be consistently carried out. Even though Jesus, with his free associations with suspect groups, did not correspond to the ideal image of the holy man, that was probably because he had long conformed to the kind of social relationships natural for a small town in Galilee. In his reaction to the hypocrisy and self-righteousness of the Pharisees from the capital city, he would certainly have met with sympathy among the people generally. Jesus was not alone in his sarcastic critique of the scribes. Rabbi Akiba, who came from the lowest stratum of society, described with bitter words how he had despised the scribes prior to his conversion.

The anti-Pharisaic position of Jesus was perhaps connected with his social background and may have been spontaneous, before it was thought through and based on principles. There is a modern misunderstanding that tax collectors were ostracized for being in the service of the occupational forces. It was the suspicion that they were involved in corruption and dishonesty, which the profession undeniably attracted, which led people to associate them with roughly the same social class as cattle thieves (shepherds!), mercenaries, and other unreliable types (cf. Luke 3:12-14). Jesus' apparent preference for "tax collectors and sinners" was, to begin with, a pointed protest against Pharisaic self-righteousness and faultfinding. But the relationship was also an expression for a basic program and that means that it is appropriate to draw this motif into our discussion.

For Jesus, tax collectors and sinners (sometimes tax collectors and prostitutes) represented "the lost sheep," those who had gone astray and must be searched for, the sick who required a physician. Jesus regarded himself as the shepherd and the physician who was called to help them (Mark 2:17 par.; Luke 15:4-10; 19:9f.). While the Pharisees regarded "sinners" as impure, who should be treated as Gentiles (cf. Matt. 18:17), Jesus emphasized that they were children of Abraham (Luke 19:9). They were sick lambs who needed to be healed, not quarantined. Jesus defended his position in several parables, primarily the parables of the lost sheep, the lost coin, and the lost son in Luke 15 (cf. also Matt. 20:1-16; Luke 7:41-43; and further Matt. 21:28-32; Luke 18:9-14). These parables in particular assume that "sinners" belong to the people of God, that they are children of the household. They are important as arguments because they show that Jesus' conduct accords with God's attitude and will. "Have I any pleasure in the death of the wicked, says the Lord God, and not rather that he should turn from his way and live?" (Ezek. 18:23).

If we want to interpret Jesus' concern for the lost in light of eschatological role models, it is appropriate to consider the expectations which were tied to Elijah the restorer. It is worth mentioning that the gospel tradition permits John the Baptist to strike a posture similar to that of Jesus. Surprisingly, the parable in Matt. 21:28-32 is linked to John. But the combination of Jesus' coarse attack on the people's leaders and the strong emphasis that the lost really belong to God's people, makes it even more appropriate to mention Ezekiel 34, a speech threatening the bad shepherds with judgment and promising rewards for the good shepherds. There appear to be several allusions to this same chapter in the Gospels (Matt. 9:36; 25:32ff.; Luke 15:4; John 10:11ff.). In Ezek. 34:23 we read: "And I will set up over them one shepherd, my servant David." We must exercise caution in claiming the presence of biblical allusions whenever terms like "shepherd" and "sheep" occur in a text, since images from pastoral life must have been familiar and natural. Yet it is reasonable to suppose that Jesus was aware of Ezekiel 34, and saw himself in the role of the new David sent by God to seek after the lost sheep, bind up the wounded (v. 16), and protect the weak ones who are pushed away by the strong (v. 21). Concern for the weak and rejected and support for those who suffer injustice belongs to the general conceptions of the messianic task in conformity to important and often emphasized aspects of the classical role of the Israelite king.

Jesus' preaching activity

A characteristic feature of Jesus' activity was that he went about from place to place to preach the gospel of the imminent coming of the kingdom of God. In all probability he labored only on purely Jewish soil. It is unlikely that he preached in Samaria, as John 4 reports. He even avoided the more important towns in Galilee, even though he often found himself operating in their vicinity. Sepphoris was situated so close to Nazareth that they probably exchanged goods and services. Tiberias lay by the Sea of Gennesaret. Perhaps Jesus classed these cities with the confederated Hellenistic cities called the Decapolis. It is also conceivable that for both practical and political reasons it would have been impossible to appear there. There are instances in which he showed mercy to unfortunate people who were not Jews, but they are striking exceptions. He was sent only to the lost of Israel (Matt. 15:24).[25]

One point of similarity between Jesus and John the Baptist is that, for each, the activity of preaching took place primarily in the open air, partly in uninhabited regions where his audience had to seek him out. Yet, in the case of Jesus, appearances are also reported in synagogues and private homes.

It is impossible to make a meaningful distinction between Jesus' public preaching and the instruction of his disciples. The tradition blends them together. We also get the impression that the instruction of the disciples often went on while large crowds were listening. The Sermon on the Mount is a prime example. The evangelists also emphasize that "secret" instruction of the disciples took place, a motif partly related to the command to silence. John is an exception (cf. 18:20), though the well-known farewell speeches of chaps. 14-17 are perfect examples of preaching in "closed meetings." The theory that Jesus spoke to people in incomprehensible parables which he later explained to his disciples in private (Mark 4:10-12, 34), is obviously an artificial construction. Yet it could have had some points of contact with reality, since it is not difficult to believe that the instruction of his disciples often had the character of discussion about the parables. It is inappropriate to speak of any "arcane discipline," i.e., a secret teaching similar to that known from Qumran. At any rate the problem is whether there was in fact a "messianic secret," i.e., instruction about Jesus' own person, particularly his suffering and death (and resurrection?), and perhaps also about the future situation of the disciples (the messianic woes). In any event one can scarcely speak of any sort of carefully guarded secret. Even the evangelists presuppose that there was a great deal of discussion about whether Jesus could possibly be the Messiah or whether Jesus regarded himself as the Messiah. Mark observes that Jesus' opponents understood the point of the parable of the unfaithful tenants only too well (12:12). But otherwise one would have to say that in the nature of the case if Jesus had looked on himself as the coming Messiah, then there must have been a messianic secret, and the evangelist's conception that Jesus, during the period following Peter's confession, began to prepare the disciples for the suffering has a probable historical basis.

The so-called controversy stories can be considered a distinctive form of preaching in which, as a rule, the opponents of Jesus (the scribes) tried to call him to account or attempted to "catch him in his words." Yet Jesus consistently drove them into a corner. Some of the parables which belong to that setting often have an obviously polemical character.

This whole activity can be characterized as "prophetic," once we understand the term in its comprehensive significance. The prophetic tradition contains analogies to all forms of the preaching of Jesus. Like the prophets, Jesus was convinced that he had been sent to Israel with a definite message from God. Just as was expected of Elijah, who would be revealed in the last days, Jesus called everyone to repentance while there was yet time. If he regarded himself as the coming Messiah, the savior king of a redeemed people, then he functioned in a preliminary way as the one anointed though not yet enthroned, actually as his own forerunner. He gathered together and prepared the people which he, as Messiah, would rule over.

It is appropriate at this point to remember the distinctive notion of "anticipation" which may be present. The "prophetic perfect" is, of course, a well-known phenomenon in which the prophet presents his predictions in terms of an event which has already taken place. For instance, he might prophesy the destruction of Jerusalem using the form of a song of lament over the ravaged and destroyed city. This form is not found among the words of Jesus, though Luke 10:18 is very close. Jesus does not speak about future events as if they had already taken place. It is more accurate to say that the future in some way becomes present, because it already seems to be represented in Jesus' person and to be realized in his words. "The kingdom of God is in the midst of you" (Luke 17:21). "Today this scripture has been fulfilled in your hearing" (Luke 4:21). "Blessed are your eyes, for they see, and your ears, for they hear" (Matt. 13:16 = Luke 10:23). The beatitudes of the Sermon on the Mount logically point to a future salvation as the basis for happiness, but blessing is already experienced by the "poor ones" who hear them pronounced. They are therefore characterized as "the salt of the earth" and "the light of the world" (Matt. 5:13-14). The parables of growth cannot really be understood in any way other than that the kingdom of God is present in and through Jesus and his disciples as seed, or germ, or leaven.

In Matthew, particularly in the Sermon on the Mount, it may appear as if Jesus is presented in the role of a new Moses, who with obvious authority prescribes an eternal, thoroughly valid Torah. Nothing, however, suggests that Jesus himself thought along such lines, even though it was assumed that whatever he said was definitive. "Heaven and earth will pass away, but my words will not pass away," we read in Matt. 24:35, and, even though it is probably not an authentic saying of Jesus, it very likely captures his own actual perspective accurately. It is worth noting that we get a completely different impression of the torah (i.e., the rules and prescriptions) of the Qumran community. Even though they considered themselves "the holy ones of the last days," claimed possession both of God's Spirit and the true understanding of Scripture, and granted unchallenged authority to the teacher of righteousness, the community expressly regarded the torah of the community as provisional, valid only until the coming of the Prophet and the anointed ones.

One aspect of the Jewish conception of the Messiah is that he will provide instruction in the true Torah. Even the ability to silence opponents with his wisdom is a royal virtue (cf. Solomon), and to that extent one can say that the controversy stories of Jesus also can be compared with messianic conceptions. Of course, Jesus did not function as the Messiah when he wandered about preaching and teaching and driving scribes to distraction. What we can say is that these activities are performed in a manner consistent with a consciousness of being the one chosen and anointed with the Spirit of God to *become* the Messiah. We can scarcely go so far as to maintain that the *form* of Jesus' preaching breaks out of prophetic categories, thereby testifying that Jesus regarded himself as something more than a prophet of the end time. In fact, such a claim can be based only on the *content* of his preaching.

Here we may add a comment on a special point. Mark 2:5 (Matt. 9:2; Luke 5:20) reports that the scribes were outraged when Jesus granted forgiveness of sins to a person, thereby usurping a prerogative belonging to God alone. Jesus maintained that he had received authority to forgive sinners (Mark 2:10). The only other example of an explicit pronouncement concerning the forgiveness of sins is found in Luke 7:48. The indirect testimony that Jesus caused people to believe that God had forgiven them is more abundant. In general it is inadvisable to place much weight on this feature as an indication that Jesus had a messianic self-consciousness. Absolution of sins on God's behalf is, in and of itself, not particularly extraordinary. The assurance of absolution was doubtless appropriate in connection with cultic purifications and sacrifices. Scripture relates that prophets could announce that God had annulled punishment (e.g., 2 Kings 20). There is evidence that Jewish charismatics promised forgiveness of sins to the sick in order to heal them. John the Baptist proclaimed the forgiveness of sins for those who confessed their sins and submitted to baptism. Whether the Pharisees were outraged over the way Jesus announced the forgiveness of sins (which was perhaps intended as a provocation to them), Jesus' conduct is completely understandable on the basis of his inner assurance of God's will to forgive repentant sinners. In itself that need not suggest that he placed himself in an absolutely unique position, even if he certainly did not think that each and every person could do what he did.

Symbolic actions

Nearly everything Jesus did was capable of receiving symbolic significance later on, and many of his acts must also have held symbolic meaning for Jesus himself (e.g., the exorcisms). Yet, in particular cases there is reason for speculating whether an action was motivated primarily by a consciously symbolic intention. The most obvious example in the tradition, the cursing of the fig tree (Mark 11:12-14,20-25 and par.), must, for critical reasons, be disregarded.[26] The miracle of the loaves must also remain outside our purview, because it cannot be determined what, if anything, constituted the historical kernel of that story. Miracles with close parallels in the Old Testament or in widely circulating legends are particularly suspect.

The triumphal entry into Jerusalem, however, merits careful consideration, as does the cleansing of the temple and the last supper. In every respect the historical problems are enormous and all conjectures regarding the intentions of Jesus are extremely tenuous. John situates the cleansing of the temple as a programmatic action at the beginning of Jesus' ministry, but, apart from the fact that it is generally risky to prefer Johannine to synoptic tradition, one cannot imagine that the authorities would have sat on their hands in the face of such a blatant provocation and let Jesus go in peace. It is difficult enough to understand how Jesus could be free for such a long time before his arrest as narrated in the synoptic Gospels. Probability suggests that the entry into Jerusalem and the cleansing of the temple belong together. In distinction from Matthew and Luke, Mark reports that the episode in the temple occurred the day following the triumphal entry, perhaps because Mark wanted to fill each day of the week with an event, or thought that the cleansing of the temple should take place early, at the busiest time of the day. Mark is possibly right, while Matthew and Luke want to pull the two events even closer together.

It is appropriate to begin with Mark, utilized by both Matthew and Luke, but we must entertain the possibility that both Matthew and Luke knew other versions from oral tradition. Further, Luke may well have used several written sources. Even though we might have good reason to doubt that the sources provide a trustworthy account of events, it is at any rate impossible to reconstruct any other sequence of events, and it is unreasonable to think that the whole account is fabricated on the basis of particular biblical texts (e.g., Zechariah 9; Ps. 118:25f.; Mal. 3:1). It is striking how little in Mark's presentation of the last days of Jesus bears telltale signs of the later perspective of the church. If one did not know better, one could almost read the report as a serious account of the dramatic course of events which resulted in the tragic end of the Galilean prophet. Actually, that indicates that the evangelist took into account the fact that the Christian reader, from the perspective of his faith, is in a position to catch the double meanings and grasp the deeper, paradoxical significance of the narrative all along. Otherwise he would not have been able to read the story of Jesus' suffering as gospel. It is, for instance, peculiar—though typical—that Mark 11 never draws attention to the fact that Jesus' entry into Jerusalem must be understood from the perspective of the messianic prophecy in Zech. 9:9 (cf. Matt. 21:5; John 12:15).

All versions of the triumphal entry exhibit a messianic character. In Mark, Jesus is not acclaimed directly and unambiguously as the Messiah, as he is in the other Gospels (Matt. 21:9, "the son of David"; Luke 19:38, "the king"; John 12:13, "the king of Israel"). The first part of the cry of acclamation (Mark 11:9 and par.) is derived from one of the "Hallel Psalms" (118:26), which were firmly rooted in the Passover liturgy. But this acclamation could read in two ways: "Blessed be he who comes in the name of the Lord," or, "Blessed in the Lord's name be he who comes." Luke assumes the latter possibility and interprets "he who comes" as "the king," i.e., the Messiah. Since Ps. 118:26 is actually a greeting from Zion to the festal pilgrims, that in itself does not imply that Jesus was proclaimed as Messiah. The second part of the acclamation (Mark 11:10a), "Blessed is the kingdom of our father David that is coming!" is also remarkably indirect, because in and of itself it only expresses the Jewish future hope by praising the blessed kingdom which will one day come. In the specific situation, however, it must imply that all future expectations are linked to the person who now rides into the holy city, and it expresses the fact that "they supposed that the kingdom of God was to appear immediately" (Luke 19:11). Matthew 21:15f. and Luke 19:39f. reproduce in different forms traditions that some of the religious leaders (Matt. 21:15, "the chief priests and the scribes"; Luke 19:39, "some of the Pharisees in the multitude") tried to get Jesus to silence those who cried out, but were brusquely refused. The implication is that Jesus accepted homage as the Messiah.

If the main features of the triumphal entry scene are historical, it can scarcely be interpreted in any way other than as a conscious, deliberate demonstration and provocation. This is the first instance, as far as we know, that Jesus used a mount. Even though an ass was not exactly a symbol of nobility and proud pretentions, but a pack animal and mount for poor people, Jesus' performance was understood as a signal to the disciples. Though it may not have been immediately understood (cf. John 12:16), it is nonetheless clear that Jesus consciously intended to fulfill the prophecy in Zech. 9:9 and by so doing indirectly make known that he was prepared to let himself be proclaimed Messiah. The inhabitants of Jerusalem and the Passover pilgrims were invited to receive him as the promised savior, while the leaders of the people were provoked into taking action. If this understanding is correct, there is a kind of programmatic symbolism in connection with this particular prophecy which conveys an unconventional image of the Messiah as a meek prince of peace who does not ride upon a proud stallion but upon a lowly ass. There is a rabbinic saying that the Messiah will come "poor and riding upon an ass" (and not on the clouds of heaven, as in Dan. 7:13), if Israel does not have any merits to display.[27] Interestingly, the focus in this instance is on the feature of the *ass*. It was thought necessary to find an explanation why the Messiah should come in such a lowly manner.

If the interpretation of the entry into Jerusalem is uncertain, the situation is even more difficult in the case of the cleansing of the temple. It is difficult to imagine that such a tradition could have originated without a historical basis, particularly since there is no appropriate Old Testament text which could serve as the point of departure for the formation of such a legend. Zechariah 14:21b is closest, but none of the Gospels alludes to it: "And there shall no longer be a trader in the house of the Lord of hosts on that day." On the other hand, it is virtually impossible to imagine the narrative as an actual historical event. How could Jesus singlehandedly clear out that exceptionally large area known as "the court of the Gentiles"? Could such a thing occur without the temple police intervening? How would it have been possible for Jesus to take up a peaceful teaching ministry in the temple precincts during the ensuing days? How can it possibly be imagined that Jesus had such complete control over his followers that he could prevent his action from developing into a violent confrontation? Could not the explanation be that Jesus, on the one hand, shocked his own followers so much that they did not dare to follow him, while the traders and merchants, on the other hand, were so afraid that disturbances could erupt that they hurried to pack up as soon as they suspected trouble? Were the police held back so as not to provoke the notorious Galileans? By all accounts, something must have happened. Jesus must have acted with provocative authority, making the temple personnel both afraid and angry. Yet they did not dare to arrest him for fear of his many followers and sympathizers, and perhaps most of all for fear of what the Romans might do if there were any signs of a possible insurrection.

Yet the central question is this: What could have led Jesus to behave in this manner? One can easily envision a completely spontaneous, emotional outburst on the part of Jesus when he could not manage to contain the loathing and indignation he felt when he witnessed such a disgraceful spectacle in the holy place. Compare, for example, how the shepherd Amos reacted to the cultic activities carried out in the main temple of the northern kingdom (Amos 4:4f.; 5:21-27; 6:4-6). There are many traditions about Old Testament prophets which could serve as models for acts of protest (Amos 7; Jeremiah 7; Isa. 1:10-17; 28:7ff.; Mic. 3:9-12; Zephaniah 3). If we are dealing with a kind of spontaneous reaction, there is then little need to inquire into the significance and purpose of such an act. But the matter is completely different if the cleansing of the temple was in fact a premeditated and carefully planned demonstration. Then the act must have been a sort of illustration of Jesus' proclamation and must have symbolic intent. Fundamentally, it is quite remarkable that the evangelists, who ordinarily could not conceive of Jesus doing anything rashly, can give us the impression of a spontaneous action motivated by righteous indignation, an expression of Jesus' consuming zeal for the house of the Lord (John 2:17). The temple had to be purified so it could serve as a place of prayer. Mark even reports that Jesus prevented people from carrying anything through the temple. For that reason Mark could not possibly have understood Jesus' act as the condemnation of the institutional temple. The temple was sacred! It is difficult to prove that any of the evangelists found a deeper symbolism in Jesus' action. One must read a good deal into the text to claim that for Luke the cleansing of the temple meant that Jesus took possession of the temple and cleansed it so that he could use it as a place for preaching.

It is difficult to derive any significance for the cleansing of the temple from what we otherwise know of Jesus and his proclamation. We are completely unprepared for the possibility that Jesus might have a positive interest in the temple and the temple cult. Characteristically, it is the cleansing of the temple which has led individual scholars to conclude that Jesus was actually a fanatical Zealot; without that episode no one would have proposed such a notion.

It is possible to regard Jesus' action as primarily a provocation and an assault on the Jerusalem priesthood and the religious elite who made a business out of religion. They are responsible for the house of prayer becoming a "den of thieves." They have violated and misused what for them should have been extremely sacred. If this is the explanation, Jesus did not carry out any "cleansing" of the temple. It is far less probable to understand his action as a prophetic warning that the entire temple will soon be destroyed (Mark 13:2).

The problem is whether Jesus' action can be construed as an expression for a more positive symbolic meaning, i.e., whether it can have some connection with his messianic calling or with eschatological expectations. It is reasonable to see the temple as the real goal of Jesus' journey to Jerusalem, perhaps primarily because it was there that the decisive confrontation must take place. But the burning questions central to this confrontation are: Who is Jesus? What is the source of his authority? With what right does he demand that people listen to him and follow him? When "the prophet Jesus from Nazareth of Galilee" (Matt. 21:11) entered into the temple precincts at the head of those who had acclaimed him and drove out all the peddlers and money changers, it then had to be asked: "By what authority do you do these things?" (Mark 11:28 and par.). Jesus did not give a direct answer. But did he give an indirect one? Who had a right to do what he did? Was it as the Messiah that he had this authority?

The answer must be sought partly in eschatological conceptions which link the Messiah to the temple, and partly in Jesus' own sayings about the temple. If we begin with the latter, where the evidence is at least very limited, we first of all have formulations which are completely unpolemical and point to an unexpected acceptance of the temple and the temple personnel. The parable about the Pharisee and the tax collector (Luke 18:10) and the exhortation in Matt. 5:23 about becoming reconciled with one's brother before bringing an offering to the altar, spring to mind, not to mention the fact that it was natural for Jesus to teach in the temple (Mark 14:49 and par.). Of particular interest is Matt. 12:3-7, where the plucking of heads of grain on the Sabbath by the disciples was defended with several arguments by Jesus. First, David presumed to do something much worse when he and his men were hungry: he went into the house of God and ate the bread of the Presence. Second, Jesus referred to the fact that the priests work in the temple on the Sabbath, and then interposed the statement, "Something greater than the temple is here" (Matt. 12:6). Finally, he quoted the biblical saying "I desire mercy, and not sacrifice." Since Mark 2:25f. has just the reference to David, and the rest is material found only in Matthew, there is always the risk of secondary expansions. Yet they are not inappropriately attributed to Jesus. They tend to imply a relativization of the significance of the temple and what goes on within it. Jesus represents something greater and more important.

Of greater interest are the sayings which treat the destruction of the temple. According to Mark 13:2 and par., Jesus predicted that the time would come when there would not be left one stone on another of the entire magnificent temple complex. There is no negative evaluation of the temple in that statement. Quite the reverse. Luke 19:41-44 reports that Jesus wept over Jerusalem, which he so fervently wanted to protect from disaster. His sayings concerning the destruction of the temple do not really appear in a different light. If this saying can be connected with Jesus at all, it must be understood only in the sense that he wanted to save it from destruction (cf. Luke 13:34 = Matt. 23:37). In such a context the cleansing of the temple could be understood, not as a warning of impending judgment, but as a last desperate appeal to let the temple function as it was intended in order to protect it if at all possible. But a very different saying which creates difficulties is preserved in several other passages. Only John 2:19 presents it as a direct saying of Jesus, and then in connection with the cleansing of the temple. When the Jews wanted to know what right Jesus had to act in such a manner, he answered: "Destroy this temple and in three days I will raise it up." The evangelist then editorializes, "But he spoke of the temple of his body." In the other passages (Mark 14:58 = Matt. 26:61; Mark 15:29 = Matt. 27:40), the opponents of Jesus quote the saying in the form of hostile testimony that Jesus was supposed to have said that he would or could destroy the temple (and rebuild a new one in three days). According to the view of the evangelists, this is a *false* accusation. The saying apparently played a prominent part in the trial of Jesus and is again mentioned in connection with the accusation of Stephen (Acts 6:14). That certainly means that the impression that Jesus had said that he would destroy the temple and rebuild it was very firmly rooted among the Jews. Christians countered this in two ways: first, by denying that Jesus had said it at all, and second, by claiming that the saying had been completely misunderstood (John 2:19-21). The observation that the witnesses did not agree (Mark 14:59) can probably be taken as an indication that Jesus' saying was reproduced in several variant forms in Jewish polemic.

What did Jesus really say? Difficulties are certainly presented both by the fact that there are differences in the various accounts and that it is the opponents of Jesus who used the saying. And they, according to Mark 14:57, were false witnesses. It is remarkable that Matthew omits the report that the witnesses were lying and disagreed among themselves, just as he omits the special expansion in Mark 14:58 which says that Jesus will destroy the temple made with hands and build another one, not made with hands. That might lead us to conclude that the lie consisted precisely in this expansion. But that conclusion is too contradictory, for the "expansion" is precisely what opens the door for a spiritualizing interpretation which could fit into the community's understanding, particularly if (with John 2:21) the spiritual temple was understood to consist of the resurrected body of Jesus or of the church (cf. Matt. 16:18; 1 Cor. 3:10-17; Eph. 2:20f.; 1 Pet. 2:4ff.). A similar conception of the community as the temple of God is found at Qumran (1QH 6.26; 1QS 5.5-7; 8.4-10; 9.3-6; CD 3.18—4.10; 1QpHab 12.3). It is something of a crux that in Mark 14:57 the evangelist quotes the saying of Jesus in the form which should be easiest for Christians to accept and at the same time denies that Jesus really said it at all. Of course, that becomes all the more remarkable if the expansion is due to the evangelist's own editorial activity. One can only wonder whether

Mark inadvertently combined two dissimilar apologetic strategies, one of which emphasized that the entire accusation against Jesus was an immoral and illegal conspiracy which made use of false witnesses, while the other consisted in an emphasis that the temple saying had been misunderstood because Jesus had spoken metaphorically. When Matthew no longer follows Mark, it can be because he is familiar with another (oral) version, but it also means that he did not think it necessary to dispute the fact that Jesus could have spoken literally about destroying the temple on Mount Zion and rebuilding it again in three days. But he obviously makes it simpler by having Jesus say: "I *am able* to . . ." (Matt. 26:61) not "I *will* . . ." (Mark 14:58), for then this saying is simply one of a series of expressions for Jesus' (and the believer's) power over the world (cf. Matt. 26:53; 17:20; 21:21f.). But at the same time, it appears as if Matthew does not see any connection between this saying and the expectations which were linked to the Messiah. For Mark, there could well have been such a connection.

Now we begin to tread on even more uncertain ground. In actuality, what role could an accusation, based on a saying that Jesus would destroy the existing temple and construct a new one in three days, play for those who wanted to eliminate Jesus? Was it so blasphemous to say such a thing? The question is whether in this roundabout way the basic intention was to undercut the claim that Jesus gave himself out to be the Messiah. The high priest's tactic could be based on the hope of convincing the members of the Sanhedrin that Jesus had precisely such intentions, for if that in itself was not punishable according to Jewish Law, it would alarm members of the Sanhedrin (cf. John 11:48-53) and provide them with a basis to denounce Jesus before Pilate. We really do not know whether the idea that the Messiah would erect a new temple was a popular conception at the time of Jesus. The situation had been much different earlier, when the temple lay in ruins or when there was only a very modest, temporary structure (cf. Hag. 2:3). Understandably, the prophet Zechariah expected that Zerubbabel, a descendant of David, would build a temple (Zach. 6:12-13). But Zerubbabel was a disappointment, and the temple which was eventually built was also a disappointment. It then naturally followed that visions of the future linked the expectations of a future Messiah together with a new and glorious temple. The Targum to Zech. 6:12 paraphrases the text in this way: "Behold, a man who is called Messiah [in the Massoretic text: "Branch"] will reveal himself and become great and build the temple of Yahweh."[28] Correspondingly, the Targum to Isa. 53:5 reads: "He will build the sanctuary."[29] When Nathan's speech to David in 2 Samuel 7 was eventually read as eschatological prophecy, v. 13 was understood in such a way that it was the obligation of David's son to build a new temple (cf. 1 Enoch 90:28f.; 4 Ezra 9:38—10:57). Clearly, such conceptions were vital during periods when there was no temple in Jerusalem of which Jews could be proud. But just before the time of Jesus, Herod the Great began the construction of a magnificent sanctuary, to the great satisfaction of most Jews. In spite of their unfriendly feelings for the Idumaean Herod, the thought that the Messiah would destroy such a temple was considered thoroughly sacrilegious. It is important to bear in mind that the idea of destroying the existing temple now became a new factor, because earlier no one had been interested in protecting the sorry substitute temple razed by Herod, even though it was 500 years old. Conceivably, the religious circles which despised and scorned Herod the most were not ready to acknowledge his temple as adequate for the messianic age, though the priests in Jerusalem were certainly not in agreement. It would be most effective if the high priest could gamble both on the fact that Jesus regarded himself as the Messiah and on the fact that he had wild ideas of razing the temple.

Nothing suggests that Jesus himself had any antipathy toward the Herodian temple. He had, in all probability, predicted its destruction (Mark 13:2), but with regret! It is not natural to conclude that such a prediction alone could form the basis of the testimony of the witnesses against Jesus. Most likely, Jesus had linked a saying about the destruction of the temple with a prophetic promise that he would shortly erect a new one which he understood metaphorically as a spiritual temple ("not made with hands"). The original form of the saying cannot be reconstructed with any confidence. Neither do we know the specific eschatological conceptions Jesus may have had in mind, and whether, for example, they could have included the idea of a temple in one form or another. The Temple Scroll from Qumran contains the notion that God himself will finally erect an eternal temple, one not built with hands. Though Revelation 21 has the motif of the heavenly Jerusalem which will descend to the earth, the idea of a new temple is nevertheless missing: "And I saw no temple in the city, for its temple is the Lord God the Almighty and the Lamb" (v. 22). It is possible that Jesus could consciously have expressed himself in such a way as intentionally to arouse associations with particular eschatological conceptions of the Messiah as temple-builder. But we cannot get beyond tenuous speculations.

The entry into Jerusalem and the cleansing of the temple were public acts with symbolic significance which were probably intended to provoke the religious leaders to take a stance regarding Jesus. And that must mean, in the particular situation and from the perspective of Jesus' conviction of his calling, that they must either accept him as Messiah or silence him. The final symbolic act, the last supper, had a distinctly private character and concerned only those who had followed him and who had acknowledged him as Messiah. In this instance Paul is an earlier witness than any of the Gospels. The version he gives us in 1 Cor. 11:23-26 is a complete Lord's Supper liturgy, i.e., a formulaic cultic text intended for recital at a regular communal celebration of the Lord's Supper. The introduction, "on the night when he was betrayed," clearly assumes familiarity with the story of Jesus' suffering. The Gospel of John lacks an account of the institution of the Lord's Supper and instead reports a completely different symbolic action, that of Jesus washing his disciples' feet. Nevertheless, on the basis of John 6, particularly in the comments following the miracle of loaves, it is evident that John was not only familiar with the cultic celebration, but has a theology of the Lord's Supper as well. Mark 14:22-25 also exhibits a liturgical character, and is almost exactly reproduced in Matt. 26:26-29. The text in Luke 22:15-20 is distinctive and uncertain from the point of view of textual criticism. The longest, best-attested text in Luke has an introduction which includes the distribution of a cup of wine in association with a saying of Jesus preceding the action normally associated with the liturgy of the Lord's Supper. The shorter Lukan version omits the final cup and so gives the impression of a form of the Lord's Supper which uses the wine before the bread (as in Did. 9:1-5). In all the Gospels the institution of the Lord's Supper is part of a longer connected account of Jesus' final meal with the disciples. We can reconstruct neither the earliest form of the church's celebration of the Lord's Supper nor the sequence of events and the words pronounced at the original meal.

Because John has Jesus die at the time when the Passover lambs are killed and so situates the last supper on the day before the Jewish Passover, many scholars dispute the fact that Jesus and the disciples ate a Passover meal at all, even if that is clearly assumed in the synoptic Gospels. It is always hazardous to prefer John as a historical source, and it is obvious that the symbolism involved in the statement that "the lamb of God, who takes away the sins of the world" (John 1:29), who died at the same time that the sacrificial lambs were slain, was the determinative factor for the evangelist. The tradition that Jesus was arrested immediately following the Passover meal is certainly correct. Then those responsible acted under pressure and set aside the usual formal and legal considerations. That often happened in Jewish history. Passover evening gave Jesus' opponents the possibility of apprehending him without causing a general disturbance. It was at a high point in the festival, for Passover evening was a critical moment; it was then that Moses had led Israel out of Egypt, and therefore it was also at that moment that the Messiah was expected to intervene. Since the Passover meal had to be eaten in Jerusalem, Jesus found himself in the city, while otherwise he would probably have spent the night with friends in Bethany. Judas gave Jesus' enemies their golden opportunity. What his motives really were, however, can no longer be determined. We can no longer discard as unthinkable the hypothesis that the betrayal was desired and even planned by Jesus himself, since the arguments pro and con must necessarily be based on psychological considerations. The Gospels clearly present the situation as though Judas acted alone with despicable motives, while Jesus saw through him and yet allowed events to take their course. Everything which occurred during the Passover meal is determined by the fact that Jesus knew that it was their final gathering before his death.

The symbolic action consisted in the fact that he, at the beginning of the meal, took some bread, broke it into pieces, and distributed it to his disciples with the words: "(This is) my body." After the meal he took the cup and sent it around with instructions that everyone should drink from it. The accompanying words are preserved in various versions. Paul has, "This cup is the new covenant in [i.e., on the basis of] my blood" (1 Cor. 11:25). Mark 14:24 reads, "This is my blood of the covenant, which is poured out for many," while Matt. 26:28 adds, "for the forgiveness of sins."

Luke 22:20 runs, "This cup is the new covenant in my blood which is poured out for you." Paul alone adds the words announcing the establishment of a new ritual: "Do this, as often as you drink it, in remembrance of me" (1 Cor. 11:25b). The words are hardly authentic, but rather reflect the fact that the community commemorated Jesus' sacrificial death by repeating the ritual acts and reciting Jesus' words.

Conceivably, the tradition has expanded the words concerning the cup in order to make the symbolic significance more precise, but in this case that means only a clarification of the symbolism conveyed by the actions and an emphasis on their obvious associations. One problem with the formulation in Mark and Matthew is the negative associations necessarily connected with the consuming of blood. By his action Jesus dedicated his death to his disciples. He gave his life for them, thereby instituting a new covenant.

The associations are determined not only by the Passover ritual, the Scriptures, and the cultic use of blood, but probably also by martyrdom traditions. During the Maccabean period the martyr was an important ideal of piety. By enduring torture and death rather than transgressing the commandments of the Law, the martyrs demonstrated what faith really was. By that means they also made themselves deserving of resurrection and, in the life to come, restitution. But by giving their lives for the Law and for Israel, they also contributed to the atonement of the sins of the people. The sufferings of the martyrs functioned as substitutionary sacrifices (4 Macc. 1:11; 6:28f.; 17:20ff.). For Christians this motif became a key to understanding the significance of Jesus' suffering and death. Jesus died for us, for our sins; he gave himself for us. Inspired by the story of Abraham's willingness to sacrifice Isaac, it took the analogous form of God giving his Son for us. The question is whether the key was already used by Jesus, whether he anticipated his death not only as unavoidable and predetermined by God, but also as the sacrifice which had to be offered for the salvation of the people and the foundation of the new covenant. The question must be answered yes, if the words of institution of the Lord's Supper are based on trustworthy historical tradition.

Basically, this would not be problematical if Jesus had regarded himself as the final prophet rather than as the Messiah. It had virtually become a dogma that all true prophets had to suffer martyrdom. After the belief in resurrection had become common, it was quite natural to think that the righteous, the perfectly pious, must suffer in this world in return for a resurrection in glory (cf. Dan. 12:1-3; Wis. 3:1-9; 5:15). Jesus had taught his disciples that the one who sacrificed his life would gain life. But could not martyrdom and Messiahship go together? There was certainly nothing preventing the future Messiah from passing through trials and experiencing the most severe tests. Moses and David had done so. But if he should be tested like Job, then he could not die, since he was destined to become the savior-king in the new kingdom. Either the certainty of martyrdom made it necessary that Jesus give up the belief that he was the Messiah (if indeed he had such a belief), or he must have harbored the daring thought that it was through death and resurrection that he would become the Messiah. It is clear how the evangelists understand the matter; nonetheless, the report of the last supper is followed by Jesus' spiritual struggle in Gethsemane, where he still sought a way to escape death (cf. Heb. 5:7). While the words accompanying the distribution of bread and wine presuppose that Jesus knew with certainty that he would die, and indeed that he saw death as the fulfillment of his work, his prayerful bout with doubt and anxiety in Gethsemane betrays the desperate hope that it might be possible to avoid the cross. Hebrews 5:7 shows that Christians were able to find an edifying motif in Jesus' struggle in prayer. Yet it would have been much easier to depict Jesus' last hours in a heroic manner, such as we find in reports about the martyrs in 2 Maccabees 7, Stephen in Acts 7, and all later acts of Christian martyrs. That is also the style which characterizes the passion narrative in John. That makes it difficult to avoid the conclusion that the disciples were actual witnesses in Gethsemane to a spiritual struggle which they could not forget. The tension in this portrayal of the last night of Jesus makes sense psychologically, and it is easier to suppose that it rests on actual experience than on imagination.

There are various features in the gospel reports about Jesus' life which suggest strong emotional fluctuations, and it appears likely that his self-understanding was developed in several phases. That does not necessarily mean that he did not much earlier understand his calling as messianic, but rather that, in earlier stages, it was really anything but certain and clear what his role as the future Messiah would demand of him and lead him into. We must not get caught up in something as hazardous as psychological analysis. But it is reasonable to ask whether there was some basis for arriving at a conviction that the one who was chosen as the Messiah must pass through suffering and death just like the true prophets and those who were perfectly righteous.

Throughout history, scholars have found a biblical basis in Isaiah 53, then in psalms such as Psalm 22, and also in a variety of other passages. The saying which Jesus pronounced after the disciples drank the wine, according to Mark 14:24, apparently alludes to Isa. 53:11-12 ("for many"). The allusion is clearer in Mark 10:45. There is no evidence that any Jew had drawn the conclusion from Isaiah 53 that the Messiah had to die to atone for the sins of the people. But if the Aramaic Targum already in the pre-Christian period preserves a traditional identification of the Servant with the Messiah, nothing stands in the way of believing that it was in Isaiah 53 that Jesus himself found the key to understand his own role as God's anointed one.

9

The Son of Man

Gospel tradition unanimously attests that on many occasions Jesus referred to himself as "the Son of man" (Greek: *ho huios tou anthrōpou*). It is quite natural to assume then, that this self-designation provides a descriptive term for what he thought of himself and his role. Both with respect to Jesus' use of this expression and its significance, however, contemporary scholars go in a number of different directions. In fact, this is the most debated topic in modern scholarly research on Jesus.

Within the context of this bewildering debate, there is one claim which I can assert with some confidence: *all theories which are based on the assumption that "Son of man" was a title in Judaism are untenable.*[30] The stumbling block for all such theories is Matt. 16:13, "Who do men say that the Son of man is?" It is clear both from the context and from the ways in which the saying is formulated in parallel passages (Mark 8:27; Luke 9:18) that the meaning is, "Who do people say that *I* am?" One of the possible answers (and the only really correct one, according to many scholars) is then logically excluded: "You are the Son of man." At least in this passage, "Son of man" replaces "I." If we do not want to believe that the evangelist erred by making an incredible slip of the pen we can confidently claim that Matthew did not know that "Son of man" could have a titular meaning. At least to him it was simply an expression Jesus used to designate himself.

Even though no one has managed to remove this stumbling block from the way, most scholars still cling to the hypothesis which was introduced by the end of the 19th century that "Son of man" was the name of an eschatological figure to which certain apocalyptic groups tied their hopes for the future. He was a preexistent, heavenly "Man" who would be revealed on judgment day and function as judge on behalf of God. Some scholars think that the idea is based on a "messianic" interpretation of Dan. 7:13, similar to that reflected in the Similitudes of Enoch (1 Enoch 37–71), which must be dated to the late first century A.D. at the earliest. Others believe the idea is older and originated in non-Jewish speculation about the primal man or myths about the gods. The conviction that this same apocalyptic title recurs in the Gospels has led scholarship into endless complications, such as the hopeless controversy over which Son of man sayings are genuine. Some scholars think that Jesus actually identified himself with the Son of man and for that reason they can accept the authenticity of all the various types of Son of man sayings. Others think that only those sayings are genuine in which Jesus does not refer to himself but expresses his own belief in an apocalyptic Son of man. Still others conclude that no Son of man sayings can be genuine, because Jesus did not at all share the apocalyptic conceptions to which the notion of the Son of man belonged. According to this view, Jesus was first identified as the Son of man by the earliest Christian community which formulated sayings of Jesus about the Son of man.

While limited space precludes detailed discussion, the critical arguments against the view that "Son of man" was a Jewish designation for an eschatological figure may be briefly summarized:

1. There is no pre-Christian evidence for the existence of a "Son of man" title.[31]

2. The "Son of man" designation does not occur in Christian confessions.[32]

3. The Old Testament texts which use the expression "Son of man" (Hebrew: *ben adam*), are not used Christologically in the New Testament.[33]

4. Jesus is not called "Son of man" by others.[34]

5. The self-designation "the Son of man" is not understood as an answer to the question of who he is.[35]

6. There is not a single Son of man saying which makes sense *only* if "Son of man" is a Jewish title.

7. There are several sayings which make reasonable sense only if Son of man is not a title.[36]

8. It has not occurred to the evangelists (or even the ancient copyists) that sayings attributed to Jesus about the Son of man that formally sound as if Jesus is speaking of someone else could actually be misunderstood in that way.[37]

9. While the apocalyptic Son of man is assumed to be a heavenly being associated with power and glory, in the Gospels the designation is often associated with earthly lowliness, suffering, and death—without being presented as either something new or contradictory.

When the idea of the apocalyptic Son of man is abandoned, the problem of the authenticity of the Son of man sayings appears in a different light. Since "Son of man" can be regularly replaced with a personal pronoun ("I" or "me"), which frequently occurs in parallel sayings in other Gospels, the Son of man sayings must be judged like other "I" sayings. Generally it can be said that the sayings which have the most prominent apocalyptic features inspire the least confidence. Apocalyptic motifs appear to have played a more pronounced role for the early church than for Jesus, and the church used Dan. 7:13 as a messianic prophecy (in contradiction to Dan. 7:18,22,27, but in keeping with a widespread Jewish exegetical tradition).

The most difficult problem is deciding whether Jesus' use of "Son of man" is anything more than an insignificant circumlocution for the personal pronoun. That people in certain contexts prefer to use a circumlocution for "I," is a widespread phenomenon. In British English, for instance, the term "one" is often preferred in such contexts. Upon receiving a prestigious award, a member of the British aristocracy reportedly responded, "One is immensely honored." A few scholars think they can demonstrate a similar use of the Aramaic expression *bar nash* ("son of man"), or *bar nasha* ("the son of man"), which they think is the basis for the Greek phrase *ho huios tou anthrōpou* ("the son of man"), an expression which sounds peculiar in Greek. The phrase merely means "person" or "the person," and is used in the Aramaic translations of the Old Testament to reproduce the Hebrew *ben adam* ("son of man").[38] We do not know whether the Hebrew expression *ben adam* was used as an indefinite pronoun, although the Aramaic idiom *bar nash* was regularly used in that way. It is also demonstrable that *bar nash,* just as the English term "one," can be used in certain contexts instead of "I," although in the evidence thus far adduced that occurs only in statements which have a more general application. If someone mortally ill should say, "There are so many things one thinks about when one just lies here like this," that actually means "I have a great deal to think about when I lie here on the point of death." Here the indefinite pronoun corresponds to situations which are typical for people who are near death. It would be unacceptable, though not impossible English to say, "Who do people say that one is?" This usage is possible only if the intended meaning is, "What do people say about one such as I?" None of the Aramaic examples goes that far. This means that Matt. 16:13 has no real parallel and cannot be explained on the basis of the indefinite use of *bar nash* to mean "one." In the case of most of the Son of man sayings in the Gospels, a general significance is precluded. *Ho huios tou anthrōpou* must mean "this person," i.e., "I and no one else." The Aramaic texts only offer parallels to the very few instances in the Gospels where "Son of man" *could* be construed as having general significance. Several examples: "So the Son of man [= man] is lord even of the Sabbath" (Mark 2:28 and par.); "Whoever says a word against the Son of man [= a man, a person like myself] will be forgiven" (Matt. 12:32; Luke 12:10); "Judas, would you betray the Son of man [= a human being] with a kiss?" (Luke 22:48). Phrases meaning "this person," whether in Greek or Hebrew, normally require the use of a demonstrative pronoun (Greek: *houtos,* "this," Hebrew: *hahu,* "this"). There do not appear to be any instances in which *bar nasha* means "this person" when lacking the demonstrative pronoun (*hahu*). That, however, could be due to the limited comparative material now available.

It is obvious that *bar nash(a)* is normally used with the general and generic meaning of "a person," "someone," "a human being [in distinction from other beings]," and occasionally with the nuance of "a normal human figure" or "an ordinary man." The expression frequently functions with the indefinite meaning "one." But this does not correspond to the use of "Son of man" in the New Testament and provides no explanation for this extraordinary Greek form of expression.

There are several theoretical possibilities for explaining the meaning of the "Son of man" designation in the Gospels:

1. In Galilee the expression *bar nasha* could have been used when "this person" (= "I") was meant. But no evidence for this usage has been found, and if it was a common idiom it is strange that it was used only by Jesus and strange also that it was not reproduced in idiomatic Greek (as, for example, *houtos ho anthrōpos,* "this person"), or simply with a personal pronoun.

2. Jesus used *bar nasha* in a way that was peculiar to him. It must have been striking and was understood as characteristic of his style. That is the reason why the expression is only used by him (or by some imitating him) in the New Testament, and that it was translated in a form which also appears peculiar in Greek.

3. Jesus called himself *bar nasha,* virtually using the expression as a name. It is constructed in a manner typical for Semitic surnames and nicknames, a fact which makes the literal Greek translation comprehensible.

The first possibility cannot be considered seriously until convincing evidence is produced. That which has been adduced thus far is inadequate. The choice between 2 and 3 is very difficult. In favor of 2 is the fact that the synoptic Gospels do not betray the slightest interest in the designation. No one wonders why Jesus uses it; no one provides an explanation. There are also other examples where singular features are preserved, such as the use of *amen* at the beginning of a statement. It can be objected that we should expect to find "Son of man" instead of "I" in all types of contexts. Why does the phrase "the Son of man says . . ." never occur?[39]

Undoubtedly, the lack of interest in its meaning speaks against the supposition that *bar nasha* (or *bar/ben adam*) served as a sort of proper name. Nevertheless, in my view, there is a play on words in John 5:27, where many English versions and translations are misleading. The RSV, for example, has: "[The Father] has given him authority to execute judgment, because he is the Son of man." Yet in this passage alone in the Gospels the designation "Son of man" lacks the Greek definite article, and should therefore be translated "because he is *a* human being."[40]

To account for the fact that Jesus can *name* himself the Son of man, several examples can be given in which Jesus himself gave nicknames to others. Simon was called *Cephas* (Greek: *Petros*), meaning "Rock" (Matt. 16:18), and the two brothers James and John were given the nickname *Boanerges,* or "Sons of Thunder" (Mark 3:17). In neither instance is a direct explanation provided. Luke 9:54 is possibly a fragmentary anecdote which tries to explain the origin of the latter nickname. Similarly, Matt. 16:18 may be an explanation (perhaps legendary) for Simon's nickname. Another important observation is that even though it is usually possible to replace "Son of man" with a personal pronoun, the designation is not used in a totally arbitrary way. *The "Son of man" designation is used when Jesus says something about himself, whether about his calling or his fate.* In some cases it is used to achieve a special effect such as a play on words, perhaps even intentional ambiguity. Such features can become more evident in a reconstruction of the underlying Aramaic form. It is unreasonable, however, to expect a consistent use of the designation, since we are dealing both with long chains of tradition involving translation into a different language and also, in many instances, with inauthentic sayings. A weighty argument that "Son of man" was used as a nickname is the fact that there are instances in which the phrase was taken up by others and used in place of the name "Jesus" (cf. Stephen in Acts 7:56).

If Jesus, in certain situations, chose to refer to himself as the Son of man in such a way that the phrase functioned as a name or a title, we cannot avoid asking what he meant by it. Perhaps the designation is symbolic, rather than incidental and immaterial, intended to evoke meaningful associations. The classical explanation, the accepted view until the present time, first occurs in John 5:27: Jesus, who was God's Son, called himself the Son of man because he had been incarnated upon the earth in human form. There is no indication that the synoptic evangelists thought along such lines, even though Luke and Matthew are familiar with the idea of Jesus' supernatural birth. Some formulaic statements in Paul's letters suggest that the Son of the eternal God revealed himself as a human being. Paul can speak of Jesus as David's son according to the flesh, and God's Son in power by the Holy Spirit (cf. Phil. 2:6-11; Rom. 1:3-4). However, it cannot be demonstrated that Paul knew and had reflected on Jesus' self-designation. It is certainly hard to believe that he had never come across the term; he must certainly have been familiar with oral forms of gospel tradition. It is unlikely that Jesus himself had similar conceptions, i.e., that he could have believed that he was an incarnation of a heavenly being, even if such ideas were not completely foreign to his Jewish contemporaries. Since the author of the Gospel of John cannot be considered a reliable historical source, no evidence suggests that Jesus thought of himself in any terms other than as a normal human being, the son of Mary and Joseph.

More recently it has commonly been supposed that Jesus derived his self-designation from Dan. 7:13. Indeed, the text speaks only of "one like a son of man," i.e., a figure in human form (often used to describe angels, cf. Dan. 8:15; 10:5,16,18). He, in contrast to the four beasts, functioned as a symbol for "the saints of the Most High" (Dan. 7:18). By the time of Jesus, the expression, in all probability, was interpreted to mean the Messiah. Nonetheless, it is by no means proved that the name "Son of man" was derived as a designation for the Messiah (or an apocalyptic parallel to the Messiah). Traditional sayings of Jesus quote or allude to Dan. 7:13 (most clearly, Mark 13:26; 14:62), but it is doubtful whether any of them are authentic. It is perfectly clear from all the evidence, including John, that "Son of man" is neither understood nor construed as a messianic title or designation. In itself, the fact that Jesus called himself the Son of man does not reveal who he is or what role he will play. The question must be put thus: *When Jesus knew that he was anointed by the Spirit of God and chosen to play the role of the Messiah of Israel, was it then of any particular significance that he described himself as the Son of man?* Does this designation reveal anything about the manner and content of his messianic consciousness?

Those who think that the Son of man designation is derived from Dan. 7:13 (directly or indirectly) assume that Jesus' messianic conceptions have an apocalyptic character, though they do not often want to take that to its logical extreme. It has often been maintained that Jesus, by calling himself the Son of man, indicated that he did not want to identify himself as a nationalistic son of David, a political Messiah. His kingdom is not of this world. But Daniel 7 cannot easily be pressed into the service of a supranational and supraworldly conception, either when the humanlike figure is correctly understood as a symbol for Israel or for Israel's Messiah. The cosmic perspective here, as in most apocalypses, serves the interests of a radical nationalism.

It is natural to look for a biblical basis for Jesus' choice of the Son of man self-designation. The use of the Hebrew expression *ben adam* in the Old Testament certainly merits consideration. Yet this phrase is but one of several expressions used to designate a human being as a type or exemplar of humanity and does not have the character of a specifically biblical term. The stereotypical formula "You, O son of man" in God's way of addressing Ezekiel certainly does not mean that God used the term *ben adam* as a *name* for the prophet (the Targum has *bar adam*). Rather, the phrase means that God continually reminds him of who he really is in relation to God— a weak and abject human being. It must be admitted, however, that the texts do not emphasize that the expression has such associations. For that matter, one could, by considering the vision in the opening chapter of Ezekiel in which God himself is seen in the likeness of human form (1:26), conclude that a human being is a creation formed in the image of God. The prophet is then reminded that he represents the human being, created in God's image. Psalm 8 combines both perspectives. On the one hand, it is incomprehensible that God should be concerned with and bother about anything so small and insignificant as human beings. Yet on the other hand, he has placed them over all other created beings, crowned them with glory and honor, and made them to be, as it were, gods upon the earth. Since none of these features is emphasized in Ezekiel, there is also the possibility that "son of man" as form of address is actually neutral. The fact that the phrase functions so differently in Ezekiel in comparison with the Gospels makes it appear artificial to search for the key to Jesus' use of the term "Son of man" in that prophetic book. In the Gospels the phrase never occurs as a form of address, but only in Jesus' descriptions of himself, and in what he says about himself. Rarely is it connected with any motif from Ezekiel.[41] The prophet Ezekiel, in short, was not a model for Jesus.

Since there is no clear indication that Jesus derived the self-designation "Son of man" from the Scriptures, we are forced to build on the significance of the phrase "Son of man" itself, and what people would have associated with it at the time of Jesus. If Jesus spoke Aramaic, but used the Hebraic form *ben adam*, or the mixed Aramaic-Hebrew form *bar adam* (as we find in the Aramaic version of Ezekiel), the self-designation would have appeared more striking and most likely called forth biblical associations with Adam. It has been argued, on the basis of the logic inherent in Mark 2:27-28, that Jesus called himself *ben adam*. According to this view, Jesus was referring to the creation account where Adam was created before the Sabbath. If the Sabbath was created for Adam's sake, it is logical that Adam's son is also superior to the Sabbath. But probability suggests that Jesus used the Aramaic equivalent *bar nasha*, the common idiom for "a human being." If Mark 2:27 provides the justification for v. 28, *bar nasha* must have been used generically: human beings (people) are superior to the Sabbath. Understood in this way, the phrase fits well in its context, where it was not Jesus but rather his disciples who came into conflict with Sabbath regulations. It is possible that a generically intended saying in the tradition could have been transformed into a word about the Son of man in a special sense, Jesus. It is also quite possible that Jesus himself capitalized on an ambiguity.[42]

It would be helpful if we could decide the extent to which the "Son of man" designation evoked thoughts of insignificance and weakness, on the one hand, or strength and power, on the other. In other words, was it a pretentious or a modest self-designation? It would be possible to proceed tentatively by either placing before the phrase "Son of man" modifiers such as "poor" or "wretched," or terms with the opposite significance, such as "himself" or "the elect." It must be admitted that it then becomes for the interpreter a matter of preconditioning, and that one's sense of what is fitting is also dependent on the understanding one already has of *bar nasha*. In some cases, the content of the sayings connect the "Son of man" designation with insignificance, weakness, and suffering, but in other cases with authority and glory. The problem is whether we can decide when it seems paradoxical to say any such thing about the Son of man. After going through all the evidence, I for my part have come to a clear conclusion: it is not really paradoxical to combine the terms *son of man—insignificance—suffering,* but all sayings about the authority and power of the Son of Man have a paradoxical ring. This is so, for the most part, apart from the probability that some sayings may not be authentic, because "Son of man" does not sound pretentious to the Christian community either, in spite of the Christological use of Dan. 7:13.[43]

The "Son of man" designation has no illustrious associations. It often appears to function as a completely neutral and fairly innocuous circumlocution of the personal pronoun. In places where it has a more pronounced position, it expresses the fact that Jesus in himself is only a powerless person, a poor, homeless person on the earth, delivered over to the pettiness and spitefulness of his fellow humans. Nevertheless, he is a person in whom God has confidence and whom he has made his instrument and servant. He has received power to expel evil spirits and the right to forgive sins. He has been called to proclaim the coming of the kingdom of God, chosen to sacrifice his life, but through that act to become Israel's savior.

Had someone else wandered about and called himself the Son of man, it would have been quite meaningless. The designation receives significance only in light of a messianic self-consciousness. It is the man who appears with sovereign authority who assumes that his words are obviously authoritative, who calls people to forsake all to become his disciples, who commands the evil spirits to go away, and who opens the door to the kingdom of God for the socially excluded and scorned—it is he who describes himself with this anonymous, unpretentious self-designation as if he only wanted to be just anybody. Yet it is not easy to decide whether there is anything basically programmatic in that. Can it imply a reservation toward the title "the son of David"? One might find that reasonable if others used that title of him. The tradition contains sporadic examples, but it seems at any rate improbable that there was any widespread tendency to call him "the son of David."[44] One can also imagine that Jesus called himself the Son of man because he was accused of pretending to be the Son of God (cf. the derision of "the righteous one" in Wis. 2:13-18). In any case, it seems most appropriate to understand the self-designation as *an expression that Jesus did not regard himself to be a person of any importance in or of himself.*

In a tradition retouched by the faith of the Christian community, it is remarkable that an observation such as Mark 10:18 (= Luke 18:19), one which has been problematic for scholars, is preserved at all: "Why do you call me good? No one is good but God alone." We will ignore the psychological explanations of this surprising reaction to the address "Good Teacher." The point is that Jesus declines a characteristic which, strictly understood, was only appropriate for God. (Actually, that is not what is surprising, so much as the fact that he reacted to such a common adjective as "good." If, for example, the adjective "holy" had been used, his reaction would have appeared normal.) No human being is good, not even Jesus. He did not want to be placed in any special class.

In this connection we should mention the saying that it is forgivable to speak contemptibly of the Son of man, but unforgivable to revile the Holy Spirit (Matt. 12:32 = Luke 12:10; here it appears that retouching is reflected in the parallel in Mark 3:28). Jesus stands as a person in no special position, and to that extent it is not more unforgivable to make derogatory remarks about him than of anyone else. The danger lies in deriding God's own Spirit, who is at work in him.

The short episode in Luke 9:51-55 about the Samaritans who do not wish to know about Jesus because he was on the way to Jerusalem can illustrate the attitude of Jesus. They deserved no punishment if they treated him as they would any other Jew.

Beyond this, it is difficult to produce evidence from the Gospels which gives expression to the fact that Jesus reacted against being categorized in a unique position, even though it can be said that he ought to be the first to exhibit the humility and lack of demands he proclaimed as an ideal. This is connected with the fact that it is always difficult to reveal personal humility when at the same time one has a mission which demands respect and recognition. The carpenter from Nazareth was God's prophet and apostle. God had placed him in a unique position, and it was decisive that people recognize that and believe in him as the one who was anointed with the Spirit. We have a related situation when Paul demands to be recognized as the apostle of Christ, but is accused of pride and personal ambition. It is much more likely that the tradition has forgotten episodes and sayings from the life of Jesus which could attest that he did not wish any honor for himself, possibly that he may have felt himself unworthy of his calling. We should not overlook the fact that the Jewish ideal of piety to a great extent appreciated such expressions of humility for God's elect (cf. Num. 12:3; Jer. 1:6). John 13 has a unique report that Jesus demonstrated the ideals of humility and service by washing the feet of the disciples. There is sufficient reason for being skeptical when John reports something which is not found in the other Gospels, but this time one should perhaps be a bit more hesitant. In fact, Luke 22:27

preserves a saying of Jesus which almost demands such a scene: "For which is the greater, one who sits at table, or one who serves? Is it not the one who sits at table? But I am among you as one who serves." For the rest, we have the decided impression that his disciples displayed the same respect and subservience which the disciples of the scribes displayed to their teachers, and that he as a consequence let himself be addressed as both Lord and Master (cf. John 13:13; Matt. 23:8). The widespread tendency to bring out Luke 22:27 as an argument against accepting Mark 10:45 as an authentic saying of Jesus is strange, considering the difficulties involved in fitting Luke 22:27 into the portrait of Jesus.[45]

Of all the Son of man sayings, Mark 10:45 is undoubtedly among those with the least claim to authenticity. It belongs with those sayings in which the insignificance of the Son of man could appropriately be understood as paradoxical: "For even the Son of man also came not (as one should have expected) to be served but to serve. . . ." But this saying need not be read in this way. Here the designation "Son of man" can simply mean "I," so the meaning simply is that since it is Jesus' lot to be a servant to people, the one who finally would sacrifice his life for them, his disciples must exhibit an attitude corresponding to his own. However, I do not think that we have in this instance a genuine example that *bar nasha* includes people generally: it is a human being's calling to serve others.[46] Mark 10:45 is on a level with the sayings which predict that the Son of man must suffer and die (Mark 8:31 and par.; 9:31 and par.; 10:33f. and par.). They have the character of a summary of what Jesus taught the disciples privately, not of actual sayings, and are characterized by having been formulated after the predicted events had already occurred. The authentic wording is hardly preserved in any of the passion predictions (though a formulation like "the Son of man will be betrayed into the hands of men" might well be authentic). In my view it is probable that Jesus prepared the disciples for the fact that he was heading for death, and it is natural that he used a circumlocution for "I" in such passion predictions (cf. Mark 2:20).

10

The Coming of the Son of Man

A considerable number of Son of man sayings speak of his future coming and revelation in power and glory. A special chapter devoted to the subject of "The Coming of the Son of Man" is necessary because here the focus of attention is not the "Son of man" designation itself, but rather the eschatological conceptions of Jesus. How far beyond his death has he been thinking, and how has he visualized his future role?

It is impossible to imagine that Jesus had no visions of what would occur following his death. In one form or another the notion of resurrection must have been part of his perspective. Yet, on the one hand, it is difficult to systematize the scattered sayings which turn on his position in the future; on the other hand, there are good reasons for questioning their authenticity. Those who think that Jesus did not have himself in mind when he spoke of the coming of the Son of man, but rather thought of a celestial being whom many Jews believed would be revealed on the day of judgment rarely have problems in believing that we are dealing with authentic sayings of Jesus. But for those who are convinced that there was no such thing as a conception of an apocalyptic Son of man current in the time of Jesus, and that Jesus spoke of himself as "the Son of man"—for them the apocalyptic sayings are those which become the most doubtful. They are clearly vehicles for the eschatological expectations of the earliest Christian community, who had identified Jesus in his future role of Messiah with the humanlike figure who comes with the clouds of heaven to assume authority over all the kingdoms of the world, according to Dan. 7:13-14. The early community not only believed that Jesus was risen, but also that he had been exalted to the right hand of God and enthroned as Messiah and that in a short time he would return to raise the dead and hold judgment, and then to lead all the righteous into the blessings of the new world. But are the conceptions of the early community (which involve much greater complications and complexities than this oversimplified sketch suggests) inspired by what Jesus himself said, or have they been placed in his mouth by that same community?

Neither of these alternatives can be accepted as completely correct. There can be little doubt that the community's image of Jesus and his proclamation has been influenced by the eschatological tension which belief in his resurrection brought about. That in turn led to the inclusion of certain apocalyptic motifs in the tradition. On the other hand, Jesus' own proclamation was determined by a corresponding eschatological tension, because his central message was that God's kingdom had come near and already was revealing itself as proleptically present through Jesus' own activity in the power of the Holy Spirit. He himself communicated these basic assumptions to the disciples; this made belief in his resurrection possible. Their eschatological expectations were not only aroused but in part formed in light of his proclamation. The problem, however, centers in his own place in the eschatological future. In the authentic proclamation of the kingdom of God we do not get the impression that Jesus occupies any special place in his view of the future. The conception of the kingdom of God is theocentric and theocratic. The Messiah is not mentioned, and the parables never make any reference to him. If one wants to show that the son in the parable of the wicked husbandmen corresponds to the Messiah, one only succeeds in aggravating the problem, for the son is murdered, so that it is impossible to give the vineyard to him after it is seized from the husbandmen. Now the situation in the kingdom of God is generally only hinted at through stereotyped images, so that one scarcely misses the mention of the Messiah. But at the same time these hints create some confusion, because many of them do not seem to correspond to the fact that the kingdom has become realized on earth, but give the impression of an otherworldly, heavenly mode of existence. A corresponding unclarity was characteristic for Judaism when belief in the resurrection of the righteous to eternal life had become widely accepted and created a hope which competed with the dream of Israel's redemption and the restoration of the kingdom of David. It would be paradoxical indeed if Jesus understood his own calling in messianic categories and at the same time adopted eschatological expectations which dispensed with messianic conceptions!

It is unsatisfying to be left with uncertain conjectures, but it is not possible to give a detailed description of the eschatological expectations of Jesus, not even to harmonize the apparent contradictions in the gospel tradition. It is not only individual sayings which point in different directions. How does the proclamation of the nearness of the kingdom of God and the imminent judgment cohere with the ethical teaching of Jesus, which, far from having the character of a temporary or "interim" ethic, fosters instead the impression of being a timeless understanding of God's eternal will for the life of people upon the earth? When "the days of the Son of man" are compared with the days of Noah, when people casually were given and taken in marriage and ignored all warning of the coming catastrophe, this gives a completely different impression from other sayings, for example, "For you always have the poor with you" (Matt. 26:11; Mark 14:7; John 12:8). The Messiah is the king of Israel, and Jesus felt himself called to save the lost in Israel; but what purpose did he have in view for God's people? Luke maintained that Jesus was the one who would deliver Israel and restore the kingdom. But does the new covenant imply that a new messianic people is founded in association with the remnant of Israel who had accepted Jesus as their Messiah? Did Jesus see himself assuming the future role of the new king of Israel, as Luke 22:29f. and Matt. 19:28 suggest? Can that be reconciled with the idea of the resurrection of the righteous, where the resurrected ones (to whom Jesus also belongs) are as the angels of heaven (Mark 12:25)? How do the parables of growth make sense when taken together with conceptions about the sudden appearance of the kingdom or of the Son of man? (Many other examples could be mentioned.) The tension cannot be relaxed by tradition-critical analysis, even though many of Jesus' sayings about the future are very probably inauthentic. The disturbing impression reflects the great variety which characterized the eschatological expectations of early Judaism. Apparently, Jesus did not feel the need to reduce them to any kind of order. That is perhaps less surprising when we consider how the tension and the complexity of Christian eschatology could be maintained throughout the history of the church, without bothering most Christians in the least.

In a fundamental way, Jesus diverged from all Jewish eschatology. That was apparently not the result of a polemical stance, but appears to have happened almost inadvertently. The political, nationalistically tinged expectations about Israel's compensation by and revenge over her pagan oppressors—the fundamental theme in Jewish dreams about the future—is totally absent. That necessarily means that for Jesus, the Messiah also represents something essentially different. He is not merely a new David. John 18:36 is correct that Jesus can be king only in a kingdom which is not of this world.

It is completely uncertain whether Jesus ever spoke of his own return. But he certainly did not think that death in any way meant the end. Luke 24:26 does not belong to the authentic words of Jesus, but is nonetheless an adequate statement of the matter: "Was it not necessary that the Christ should suffer these things and enter into his glory?" Again, though we do not have in Mark 14:62 the actual wording of Jesus' answer to the high priest's question, nevertheless the saying that from now on they will see the Son of man at the right hand of the Almighty may be an authentic indication of the direction of Jesus' hope. "The very stone which the builders rejected has become the head of the corner" (Mark 12:10 and par.).

11

The Suffering Servant of the Lord

The question marks have been piling up throughout this study. If a question mark had been placed after the title of this chapter, scholars would have understood the reason. "The suffering servant of the Lord" is a designation biblical scholars use for the unknown person mentioned in the poem found in Isa. 52:13—53:12. The early church read this passage as a mysterious and previously misunderstood prophecy of the true Messiah, Jesus. However, if we take into account the fact that this text was, so to speak, the oldest Easter gospel of the church, the key for unlocking the meaning of the cross, we can not help wondering about many of the citations and allusions to this passage which occur in the New Testament, because it might appear as if the point was missed (cf., e.g., Matt. 8:17). It is perhaps even more surprising that the quotations are not found where they might well have been expected. But the really unanswered question is whether Jesus himself found his role prescribed in the Servant Songs of Isaiah. That we miss references to Isaiah 53 in the sayings of Jesus cannot, however, provoke the same amazement as the scant number of quotations and vague allusions to Isaiah 53 in Paul.

There is no way of determining whether or not Jesus experienced stages of development in his self-understanding. Even though his ministry was very short, it was certainly dramatic enough to allow room for several developmental phases. The tradition is not unfamiliar with crises and decisive moments. Jesus' calling at his baptism is followed by the temptation in the wilderness. Peter's confession is followed by his attempt to seduce Jesus into avoiding suffering. The institution of the new covenant at the last supper is followed by Jesus' spiritual struggle in prayer at Gethsemane.[47] There is also evidence of pronounced emotional swings, from exuberant enthusiasm to profound disappointment, tears, and anxiety. Jesus' messianic self-consciousness may have been achieved through struggle. It must have been a struggle not only to follow his calling, but to understand its meaning. For that matter, we can imagine that the question at Caesarea Philippi was, at its deepest level, and in a very real sense Jesus' own question: "Who am I?"

Why did Jesus leave Judea and turn back to Galilee? Why did he not continue John's ministry of baptizing converts? How did he react to John the Baptist's death? Why did he go to Jerusalem?

Clearly, there was a series of decisions and turning points in Jesus' ministry. It is not obvious that he knew with complete assurance from the time of his baptism that he was anointed to be the Messiah, although there are strong arguments for that view. It is very likely that the messianic role changed for Jesus, both in content and in perspective. Mark presents the scene at Caesarea Philippi as a great turning point. From then on, Jesus began to initiate the disciples into the mystery of suffering. It is conceivable that there was an earlier phase, when Jesus himself did not actually anticipate his own suffering and death. The Gethsemane tradition strongly suggests that, until the very last, Jesus had difficulties comprehending that it was the will of God that he suffer martyrdom.

If this is correct, he cannot initially have identified himself with the Suffering Servant of Deutero-Isaiah. That also suggests that he did not begin his activity with a simple prophetic self-consciousness, since martyrdom was the lot of the true prophet, if not his distinguishing feature. If he began with the conviction that he was the promised Messiah, it is reasonable to assume that martyrdom was not part of his initial expectation. At the outset he probably cherished messianic dreams which did not become realities. When it became evident that his path led toward crucifixion, it is likely that Isaiah 53 made it possible for him to maintain the conviction that he was the Messiah. Without the aid of the Scriptures he could not have done it. Arguments that the Servant Songs were at that time understood as prophecies of the Messiah can be proposed. Even though such an interpretation immediately provoked scribal attempts to explain away the statements about the Servant's death, nevertheless the texts themselves were available to anyone able to read. We must also suspect that it was not simply exegetical artifice which led to the Servant being interpreted as a designation for the Messiah.[48] Isaiah 53 paints an ideal picture of the righteous one who suffers undeservedly and gives his life as an atoning sacrifice for many others. That served to give significance to the martyrdom of the pious. The text also speaks of subsequent exaltation and divine restitution. The Messiah represented the religious and moral ideal; he was the completely righteous one who was able to withstand all temptations and endure the most difficult tests. The one bold step which had to be taken completely to identify the Messiah with the Servant was to accept the fact that the way to messianic glory was not only to endure testing but also to pass through death to resurrection. If no scribe felt himself compelled, through quiet reflection, to take that step and think such a shocking thought, in Jesus' situation that step would have been both consistent and logical.

If Jesus, on the basis of his family tradition, could trace his lineage back to David (a possibility which cannot be excluded, despite the artificial and awkward genealogies in Luke 3 and Matthew 1), there is reason to believe that *it was both obvious and natural for him to understand his divine calling as his selection as Messiah.* One could even go so far as to emphasize that it must have been a moral obligation for every boy thought to belong to the house of David to consider himself as one who might possibly be destined "to raise up the booth of David that is fallen" (Amos 9:11).[49]

While we cannot completely avoid psychological arguments, we nevertheless want to try to anchor them in historically reasonable fixed points. The most incontrovertible facts about the life of Jesus include his baptism by John, his crucifixion by the Romans, and his proclamation as Messiah by early believers. *There is a logical consistency in these facts if Jesus, who belonged to the house of David, experienced a religious calling through his baptism which*

implied not only that he received a prophetic message to proclaim
that the kingdom of God stood just outside the doors, but also that
he himself was destined to be the Messiah. It is not simply that the
possibility that he might be the Messiah had dawned on him, but
that it was a truth revealed to him which he had to grasp and hold
on to, whatever the cost might be. Therefore, he could not, without
denying his own calling, respond with anything but a yes to the
direct question posed by the Sanhedrin. Yet, to maintain belief in
his messianic call must have been extremely difficult. Even if the
story of the temptation of Jesus is an edifying legend which may
have a very loose connection with the actual personal experience of
Jesus, it symbolizes a struggle which was very real. The temptations
have a messianic character, and give symbolic expression to the fact
that Jesus had to take a stand and reject as diabolical every showy
and self-seeking use of his position as Messiah ("God's Son"). The
scene with Peter, after he had acknowledged Jesus as the Messiah
and Jesus had begun to prepare the disciples for the fact that he must
sacrifice his life, certainly has a basis in historical fact. From a
psychological perspective, the stern rejection of Peter must be understood as an indication that Jesus really felt himself tempted and had
to struggle first to choose and then to follow the path which God
had pointed out to him, a way which deviated radically not only
from everything that Peter and the other disciples could imagine to
be the appropriate path for the Messiah, but perhaps even from the
conceptions which Jesus himself had once adhered to. Jesus' struggle
in prayer at Gethsemane, then, was the final struggle, not only with
the unwilling flesh, the natural fear of suffering and death, but with
all the doubts and with all the protestations which arose out of the
whole constellation of messianic ideas and expectations he had
turned his back on. Jesus' acceptance of the messianic calling had
become a rejection of most of the traditional conceptions which Jews
associated with the longed-for ideal king. This is scarcely comprehensible without making the assumption that he found a messianic
model in the Suffering Servant of the Lord. By that I do not mean
simply that it was Isaiah 53 alone which determined his direction
and led him to choose the path which culminated at Golgotha. This
path was, on the whole, the consequence of the religious and ethical
ideals of Jesus and the opposition he experienced from religious
leaders. It was the way of the true prophet, the pious righteous one,

which John the Baptist himself had followed. *But Isaiah 53 made it possible to believe that this was also the way for the anointed of the Lord, that the Messiah himself must suffer in order to enter into his glory.* We can say in addition that if a role model was found in the songs of the Servant of the Lord, it is easy to understand that the vision of the future did not extend beyond the hope of resurrection and exaltation. *But the consequence was that the center of gravity in the messianic role for Jesus himself shifted to that which actually became the great preparatory test: suffering and death. That became the real messianic task.* The Son of man had come to serve and to give his life as a ransom for many.

12

Epilog

We are now at the end of our journey, a path with many twists and turns. We have not always found satisfactory answers to our questions. Some answers were different from what I would have expected beforehand. That is also partially true of the main conclusion itself. Even if I cannot guarantee that it is absolutely correct, to me it appears satisfying and clarifying. Yet there is always the danger that the questions which are asked and the way of proceeding might predetermine the goal of the investigation in such a manner that perspectives and points of view which might have led in different directions are ignored. Our conclusion is neither overly sensational nor original. That in itself should be somewhat reassuring, for in this area the probability is that that which is most original is also the most mistaken.

Among the issues which remain unsolved is the matter of baptism. John baptized, and Jesus submitted to his baptism and defended both John and his baptism to the end. The early church reintroduced baptism as baptism in the name of Jesus. But there was a short intervening period in which baptism was not practiced. How do these factors fit together? We can answer that it was precisely Jesus' presence which made baptism superfluous. John baptized to prepare the people to receive the Messiah. The Christian community baptized in the name of Jesus because the Messiah had been on the earth, but had ascended to heaven. As long as he was present himself, however, baptism was irrelevant. The forgiveness of sins, salvation, and the kingdom of God were actually in their midst. Not until later was there a need for symbols which could represent him. Then came the sacraments. This answer is not completely satisfying, however, because it appears too theologically speculative. It is based on more than exegesis and historical analysis. We must admit that we do not know why Jesus thought it superfluous to continue to baptize after John the Baptist was forcibly removed from the scene. It *could* be an important indication that Jesus came with something radically new. Baptism had its time until Jesus and no longer. Jesus made it superfluous. Was that because he was the Messiah?

William Wrede made the "messianic secret" into a key word in gospel research.[50] His thesis was that the Christian community (particularly as represented by Mark) solved the problem that Jesus had never presented himself as the Messiah. The community used the theory that Jesus had consciously kept his identity secret, because it would have been impossible to comprehend what it would mean to be the Messiah until after his death and resurrection. But the actual historical explanation, according to Wrede, was that Jesus had never regarded himself as the Messiah.

My conclusion is that Mark was essentially correct. What occurred at the baptism was that Jesus experienced a prophetic calling which, in his case, because he was a descendant of David, was understood as a call to be the Messiah, "anointed" by the Holy Spirit of God. *For one who was descended from David, the Messiah was a given category for divine selection.* Inextricably interconnected and interwoven with Jesus' messianic call was the prophetic message that the kingdom of God was near. *How near it was is evident from the fact that the Messiah had already been chosen.* As *messias designatus* ("Messiah elect") he had to proclaim the gospel that the kingdom was imminent. That did not involve the necessity that he should or could proclaim himself as the Messiah. The true Messiah does not proclaim himself. He could only try to realize his secret destiny, live up to his call, do what God ordered him to do, speak with the insight given him by the Spirit, carry out those tasks which he had the power and right to perform. In this way his deeds would testify on his behalf.[51] When God had first opened the eyes of Jesus' closest disciples, so that they were in a position to believe that Jesus was the Messiah (Matt. 16:17), Jesus could then entrust them with the messianic secret to the extent that they were able to understand it. The depth of the messianic secret was such that the disciples were in no position fully to comprehend it until after the death and resurrection of Jesus. But was not Jesus actually in much the same position himself? We naturally do not have any biographical material which puts us in a position to map out in detail the development of the messianic understanding of Jesus. There are indications, however, that he experienced crises and inner turmoil and that he was compelled to make fateful decisions. They revolved around his calling and fate, around what it implied to have the role of Messiah placed upon his shoulders. A series of indirect testimonies reveals part of what he connected with his messianic calling (though these cannot be used to reconstruct the development of that calling). Since nothing is preserved which indicates that he ever had Zealot sympathies or thought along political or military lines (and that should not be surprising in one who had been converted by John), we can assume that these aspects of the messianic image had faded out earlier. Instead, we meet an unceasing struggle to restore and to heal, to drive out Satan and all unclean spirits, and win back the lost, give hope and joy to all who were social outcasts, restore God's promise in its original purity, and form a new desire to live in obedience to God and in forgiving love toward one's neighbor. We can, among other things, think specifically of the answer which was intended to quell the doubts of John the Baptist. What is mentioned is that which provided evidence to Jesus that the kingdom of God was among them and that he himself was the one who would come. We have not been able to decide how much is contained in the distinctive self-designation "Son of man," but have found it credible that it says something about a Messiah who does not want anything for himself and does not demand anything for himself, but wishes only to be a serving fellow human being and an obedient tool of God. Whether he actually was prepared for opposition and testings from the very first, it is probable that the notion that he must die, that it was his calling to give his life, must at first have been completely novel. It was, most likely, a recognition that matured later.

And, very probably, it was the songs about the Servant of the Lord in Isaiah which made it possible for him to reconcile the messianic idea with the motif of the sufferings of the innocent righteous one and the martyrdom of the true prophet. By accepting the Servant as a model for the Messiah, Jesus not only could understand that he could take upon himself the task of martyrdom even if he were the Messiah, but was able to look upon his suffering and death as the very sacrifice he had to make *precisely because* he was the Messiah. His martyrdom received significance as a means of atonement, a sacrifice which laid the groundwork for the covenant, and again as the test which qualified him for resurrection and exaltation.

We cannot *prove* that Isaiah 53 played this central role in the messianic self-understanding of Jesus. We have undertaken a reconstruction which to a large extent is an experiment in speculation. For me the resulting picture has meaning. Whether it will prove convincing to others, I have no way of knowing. If my proposals could inspire someone to work out a more adequate solution, then I have not pondered this matter in vain.

Notes

1. I have justified my criticism in an article entitled "Enthalten die Segenssprüche 1QSb eine Segnung des Hohenpriesters der messianischen Zeit?" *Studia Theologica* 31 (1977): 137-45.
2. The obscure composition about Melchizedek (11QMelch), of which fragments were found at Qumran, provides evidence, it is true, for a kind of speculation about him prior to that found in Hebrews 6, but otherwise has little in common with Hebrews and sheds no light on its Christology. It seems likely that Melchizedek in 11QMelch has either become identified with Michael, Israel's guardian angel, or the name, meaning "king of righteousness," may simply signify the Messiah, with no reference at all to Gen. 14:18.
3. More evidence can be found in my article, "Das Dogma von der prophetenlosen Zeit," *New Testament Studies* 19 (1972–73): 288-99.
4. Dial. 8.4: "But the Messiah—if he is actually born and exists anywhere—is unknown, and does not even know himself, and has no power until Elijah come to anoint him, and make him manifest to all."
5. Sigmund Mowinckel, *He That Cometh,* trans. G. W. Anderson (Nashville: Abingdon, 1951), pp. 256, 330-32.
6. Bar Kosiba is better known as Bar Kochba, meaning "son of the star." The latter designation was a nickname based on Rabbi Akiba's application to him of the messianic prophecy in Num. 24:17. Bar Kosiba, his actual name, is now known from ancient letters discovered in Palestine containing his personal signatures!

7. In the so-called Pseudo-Clementine literature of Jewish Christianity, the title *prophet* is dominant, even though it does not supplant the Messiah. The figure of the prophet is connected with a kind of incarnation idea. The true prophet, who was already present in Adam, had revealed himself several times in history; the last and most complete instance was in Jesus. As distinct from Moses, however, Jesus is not only an incarnation of the prophet, but also the Messiah.

8. See particularly Klaus Berger, "Die königlichen Messiastradition des Neuen Testaments," *New Testament Studies* 20 (1973–74): 1-44.

9. The text is cited by J. Fitzmyer, "The Contribution of Qumran Aramaic to the Study of the New Testament," *New Testament Studies* 20 (1973-74): 393.

10. Nils A. Dahl, "The Crucified Messiah," in *The Crucified Messiah and Other Essays* (Minneapolis: Augsburg, 1974), pp. 10-36.

11. The following interpretation is linguistically possible: "The one who is younger than he in the kingdom of God," namely, Jesus, who was baptized by John and in that respect came later. In the mouth of Jesus such a statement about himself appears unlikely. One must then rather believe that the addition was secondary. But it is more probable that the meaning could be to remember that the kingdom of God is more important and more glorious than everything in this world. It is more important to squeak through the gates of the kingdom of God than to be the greatest person here on earth.

12. Olof Linton, "The Parable of the Children's Game," *New Testament Studies* 22 (1975–76): 159-79.

13. The probable explanation is that the text in Mark has been corrupted. My conjecture supposes that that resulted from the fact that the text originally used the expression "son of man" of Elijah, while a copyist thought that the "Son of man" had to be Jesus and tried to alter the wording to fit that view. The Greek text in Mark 9:12b conceivably read: *'Ēlias men elthōn prōton apokathistanei panta kathōs gegraptai epi ton huion tou anthrōpou:* "Elijah comes first and restores all things, as it is written about the son of man." Mark 9:12c ("that he should suffer many things and be treated with contempt") is a secondary addition occasioned by the misunderstanding. It is possible that the reason why Luke left the section out was that the text had become virtually incomprehensible. Yet Matthew chose to reedit it and give it a comprehensible form. All speculations based on the view that Luke did not want to go along with the identification of John with Elijah must be rejected as unfounded, on the basis of Luke 1:17.

14. In and of itself one might think of the obvious parallel in the prophetic duo Elijah/Elisha. If John is a new Elijah, then Jesus can be a new Elisha, for it is told of him that he inherited a double portion of the spirit of Elijah (2 Kings 2:9f.). Things are reported about Jesus which are similar to the Elisha traditions in 2 Kings 4–5. But Elisha was too much of a counterpart to Elijah and in Jewish consciousness stood in his shadow. Since it was Elijah who was taken alive into heaven, it was thought that he would return. A new Elisha had no place in eschatological expectations. Add to this the fact that Elijah and Elisha were two of the same type, while Jesus was very different from John.

15. Nils A. Dahl, *The Crucified Messiah and Other Essays,* pp. 10-36. In a postscript (pp. 161-66), Dahl replies to my objections to the idea that there could have been other eschatological roles which might better have suited Jesus (cf.

my article "Var det noe alternativ til Messias?" *Svensk Exegetisk Årsbok* 37-38 (1972–73): 21-34.

16. See especially Joachim Jeremias, *The Prayers of Jesus* (Philadelphia: Fortress, 1967), pp. 11-65. For a more succinct summary of the views of Jeremias, see his *New Testament Theology: The Proclamation of Jesus,* trans. John Bowden (New York: Scribners, 1971), pp. 61-68.

17. C. H. Dodd, *The Parables of the Kingdom,* rev. ed. (New York: Scribners, 1961), pp. 96-102.

18. Joachim Jeremias, *The Parables of Jesus,* rev. ed., trans. S. H. Hooke (New York: Scribners, 1963), pp. 70-77.

19. Several Greek constructions, more or less synonymous, are involved, primarily combinations with *heneken,* "because of," "on account of," "for the sake of" (Matt. 5:11; 10:18,39; 16:25; 19:29; Mark 13:9; Luke 21:12), and the phrase *dia to onoma mou,* "because of my name" (Matt. 10:22; Mark 13:13; Luke 21:17).

20. The paragraph may have an authentic origin in a saying such as Luke 6:46, "Why do you call me 'Lord, Lord,' and not do what I tell you?" While Matt. 5:21 alludes to the Christological *kyrios* ("Lord") confession, in Luke the saying can concern people who formally address Jesus as "rabbi" without taking his proclamation seriously enough.

21. The traditional parable appears embellished with an allegorical interpretation of the kind found in Mark 4:14-20. It is scarcely probable that Jesus would make an allegory about the effects of his proclamation.

22. The saying occurs in a series of variant forms; cf. Mark 8:38; Matt. 10:32f.; Luke 9:26; cf. 2 Tim. 2:12; Rev. 3:5. Most scholars think that Luke 12:8f. stands closest to the original form. Actually to reconstruct an original form, however, is mere guesswork.

23. Cf. Rudolf Bultmann, *The History of the Synoptic Tradition,* trans. John Marsh (New York and Evanston: Harper and Row, 1963), pp. 112, 128, 151; similarly Rudolf Otto, *The Kingdom of God and the Son of Man,* trans. F. V. Filson and B. L. Woolf (London: Lutterworth, 1943), p. 163; Ferdinand Hahn, *The Titles of Jesus in Christology,* trans. Harold Knight and George Ogg (New York and Cleveland: World, 1969), pp. 28-31.

24. The Greek term *apostolos* is used in the New Testament (not in classical Greek) of a "sending out," and corresponds to the Hebrew *shaliaḥ.* In Mark 9:37 the verb *apostellein* ("to send out") is used of God's sending out of Jesus. The tradition of the sending out of the Twelve can provide a trustworthy explanation for the fact that they were called *apostles.* It is not thereby excluded that the term could be used of others, e.g., community delegates.

25. Among other things, the point of the stories is to put the Jews to shame. Gentiles can exhibit great faith (Matt. 8:10; 15:28; cf. Matt. 11:20-24); by the thankfulness he expressed a Samaritan leper stood out from the group of Jews with whom he had been healed (Luke 17:11-19). Jesus gave a Samaritan a starring role as one exhibiting true neighborliness in contrast to the priest and Levite (Luke 10:25-37).

26. Whatever might have been the basis for the story can no longer be determined. A dead fig tree by the side of the road might have sufficed to form the basis for a legend. Even a parable might have been transformed into a story about Jesus, or a prophetic pronouncement such as "No one will ever again eat the

fruit of this tree" (i.e., the judgment of Jerusalem will occur before the next fig harvest). All such speculations are equally plausible and equally fruitless.

27. Hermann L. Strack and Paul Billerbeck, *Kommentar zum Neuen Testament aus Talmud und Midrasch,* 5th ed. (Munich: C. H. Beck, 1969), 1:843.

28. Strack and Billerbeck, 1:94.

29. Strack and Billerbeck, 1:482.

30. My main contribution to New Testament scholarship revolves about this theme. See "Der apokalyptische Menschensohn ein theologisches Phantom," *Annual of the Swedish Theological Institute* 6 (1968): 49-105. In more succinct form, "Exit the Apocalyptic Son of Man," *New Testament Studies* 18 (1971–72): 243-267, and "Er den apokalyptiske menneskesonn en moderne teologisk oppfinnelse?" *Norsk Teologisk Tidsskrift* 70 (1969): 221-235. Several scholars, particularly those outside Germany, maintain that there was no apocalyptic Son of man title. These include, among others, Norman Perrin, E. Schweizer, J. Fitzmyer, G. Vermes, M. Mueller, B. Lindars, M. Casey. Yet they all go in different directions to solve the problem of the Son of man designation in the New Testament.

31. It is only in 1 Enoch 37–71, the so-called Similitudes of Enoch, that scholars have thought to detect the title. For reasons I have mentioned, this document cannot be adduced as evidence for otherwise unknown pre-Christian conceptions. At the most one could say that the Similitudes show us how it might be possible for a titular use of Son of Man to arise from the messianic interpretation of Dan. 7:13.

32. This is an important observation which has always been puzzling for those who regard Son of man as a title.

33. Hebrews 2:6-7 is no exception, for it is not the phrase "son of man" which interests the author in the citation from Psalm 8. However, it is possible that this citation has blunted the attention of scholars to the fact that this is an important argument.

34. Here Acts 7:57 is an exception, but Stephen does not use "Son of man" as a title, but as a designation for Jesus (cf. v. 55). In addition, Luke has in mind a reference to the saying of Jesus in Luke 22:69.

35. Cf. Matt. 16:13; John 12:34.

36. Most clearly Matt. 16:13, but see also Matt. 12:32 = Luke 12:10; Luke 11:30; 17:22.

37. The sayings about the coming of the Son of man have such a form that it appears as if Jesus speaks of someone other than himself. If the evangelists had dreamed that they could be so misunderstood, they could easily have guarded against such an eventuality.

38. There is an interesting exception in Ezekiel, where *ben adam* is a stereotypical expression used in God's speeches to the prophet, but which is reproduced in the Targum to Ezekiel as *bar adam,* which can only be understood as a reference to Adam's son.

39. This is noteworthy, since circumlocution is so often used in this way: "The king says," "the president holds," etc. This idiom is common when important people state their opinion.

40. The meaning in the context is: because Jesus is the Son of God he has power to execute judgment (vv. 21f.). Because he is a Son of man, a human being, one who "knew what was in man" (John 2:25), he has the moral right to judge

people. In a Jewish document, the Testament of Abraham 13:3, this statement is found: "For God said, 'I do not judge you, but every man is judged by man.' "

41. Allusions to Ezekiel 34 were discussed above, pp. 133-134.

42. Mark 2:10 (and par.) does not permit a generic signification, even though the conclusion in Matt. 9:8 says that people praised God who had given such power to humans. By performing an exceptional miracle, Jesus demonstrates the right of the Son of man to forgive sins. However, the point is not that Jesus is entitled to this right because he is the "Son of man," but because this person, Jesus, though he is simply a human being, has received authority to mediate God's forgiveness. "The Son of man" could here, as in most other passages, be replaced with "I" (v. 28 is the major exception), but then we would miss a point, namely, that it is a paradox that a *man* can forgive sins, for Jesus would naturally agree that "no one other than God" (Mark 2:7) can do that.

43. There are reasons for some caution. "Son of man" seemed to the Christian community to be a name for Jesus, and Jesus had become the obvious authority since he had become both Lord and Messiah. What was associated with Jesus was also naturally linked to the Son of man. For example, it is possible to speak of "the kingdom of the Son of man" (Matt. 13:41), a formulation which is inconceivable on the lips of Jesus. "The day of the Son of man" (Luke 17:24), which is the day when the Son of man (i.e., Jesus) reveals himself (v. 30), but not the day when he reveals himself as the Son of man, is also a secondary conception. However, Luke 17:22 might very well be an authentic saying, if we ignore the fact that Luke places it in a context which gives mistaken associations. What Jesus means by "the days of the Son of man," is the time he is together with his disciples before his death, not the time when "the Son of man sits upon his throne." Jesus prepares the disciples for future distress, which would become so difficult that their fondest wish would be to experience once again one of the days when Jesus was with them, even though that was also a time of trial.

44. See Matt. 9:27; 15:22; 20:30. If it was known that Jesus was a descendant of the house of David, the nickname "son of David" could have been used without having any direct messianic significance (cf. Matt. 1:20). But the evangelists certainly would have understood it messianically (cf. Matt. 21:9,15).

45. It might be tempting to reconstruct an attractive Gospel harmony by placing together the sayings in Luke 22:27 and Mark 10:45, appropriately located following the episode John describes in 13:4ff.! If we resist that temptation, we must admit that Luke 22:27 has no suitable context. Then it can have significance only if it is the Messiah who speaks to people (cf. Phil. 2:7: "taking the form of a servant"), not Jesus to his disciples.

46. This view is represented by M. Casey, *Son of Man: The Interpretation and Influence of Daniel 7* (London: SPCK, 1979), pp. 224-239. He thinks that only those sayings are authentic which use the designation "Son of man" with a generic meaning, even though they actually have Jesus in view, for then they correspond to a notorious use of *bar nasha* in Aramaic. Casey finds such sayings in Mark 2:10,28; 8:38; 9:12; 10:45; 14:21; Matt. 8:20=Luke 9:58; Matt. 11:19=Luke 7:34; Luke 12:8; 22:48. I myself find the generic interpretation improbable in the majority of instances, and do not think that Casey's solution

of the Son of Man problem is convincing. Moving in the same direction as Casey is B. Lindars, *Jesus, Son of Man* (London: SPCK, 1983).

47. This corresponds to the angels' strengthening of Jesus after the first temptation, the revelation of Moses and Elijah after the second, and, according to Luke 22:43, another instance of a strengthening angel in Gethsemane

48. The Targum replaces the name "Branch" with "Messiah" in Zech. 3:8; 6:12; Isa. 4:2; Jer. 23:5; 33:15. Zechariah 3:8 reads: "Behold, I will bring my servant the Branch [Targum: Messiah]." Therefore "my servant" means "Messiah." It follows that "my servant" can also mean "the Messiah" in other texts as well. It fits well in Isa. 42:1, and also in Isa. 43:10 and 52:13, when these verses are read out of context. It is remarkable that Isa. 53:11 is not similarly understood in the Targum that we have. See P. Seidelin, "Ebed Jahwe und Messiasgestalt im Jesajatargum," *Zeitschrift für die Neutestamentliche Wissenschaft* 35 (1936): 194-231.

49. Even though the story about Jesus as a 12-year-old child in the temple is legendary, it suggests that very early on Jesus must have stood out as exceptionally gifted. That provided both his parents and others who believed in his Davidic ancestry reason to speculate about what he might become. One day a Jewish woman would surely bring the Messiah into the world. If it was generally known that the prophet from Nazareth was a descendant of David, it is historically conceivable that he could have been given the nickname "David's son," without directly implying that he was identified with the Messiah (who is almost never described as "David's son" in Jewish texts), but rather that people had high hopes for him.

50. William Wrede, *The Messianic Secret*, trans. J. C. G. Greig (Cambridge and London: James Clarke, 1971; originally published in German in 1901).

51. Cf. John 5:31,36; 10:25. The fact that John may not preserve authentic sayings of Jesus poses no particular obstacle. The point is that the Messiah must be legitimated by God through the message and the deeds which God entrusted to him.

Glossary of Selected Terms and Abbreviations

Antiquities, a history of the Jews from the creation of the world up to ca. A.D. 75, written by Josephus (see below).

1 Enoch refers to the Ethiopic Apocalypse of Enoch (attributed to the Enoch mentioned in Gen. 5:18f.). This complex document is associated with the so-called Old Testament Pseudepigrapha (literature written under pseudonyms). It is a composite work, attested in "complete" form only as part of the Bible of the Ethiopic Church. Aramaic fragments of all portions of the book are attested at Qumran, with the exception of the section most important for our purposes, the Similitudes (chaps. 37–71). In this section, three Ethiopic expressions occur, all of which may be suspected of being reproductions of the Greek term customarily translated "Son of man."

Epistle of Barnabas is a Christian tractate from the early second century A.D., a part of the "Apostolic Fathers."

4 Ezra (= 2 Esdras), an apocalypse which probably originated at the same time as the Revelation of John, and which is part of the Old Testament Apocrypha (writings included in the Greek Bible, the Septuagint, but excluded from the Hebrew canon of Scripture). Preserved in Latin, but originally composed in Hebrew.

Gospel of Thomas, a collection of sayings of Jesus discovered in 1945 in a Coptic translation at Nag Hammadi in Egypt, but previously known in part from Greek fragments. It has a Gnostic character and little historical value as a source for the teachings of Jesus.

Josephus, Jewish historian of the first century A.D., whose works, especially *Jewish War* and *Antiquities of the Jews,* shed light on the history of New Testament times.

LCL, the Loeb Classical Library (Cambridge, Mass.: Harvard University Press).

Mishna ("teaching"), the earliest part of the Talmud, a collection of rabbinic traditions and interpretations of the Torah from ca. A.D. 200.

OTP, The Old Testament Pseudepigrapha, ed. James H. Charlesworth, 2 vols. (Garden City, N.Y.: Doubleday, 1983, 1985). The Pseudepigrapha are Jewish writings, often in biblical style, dating from the first few centuries B.C. and A.D. which were excluded from the Hebrew as well as the Greek canon of Scripture.

par. after a reference to one of the Gospels means that there are parallel texts in the other synoptic Gospels (Matthew, Mark, and Luke).

Psalms of Solomon, a collection of 18 psalms extant in Greek and Syriac translations. Originally composed in Hebrew, probably in Pharisaic circles, shortly after the Roman occupation in 63 B.C.

Qumran scrolls. The more extensive manuscripts are designated in scholarly literature with the number of the cave in which they were found and an abbreviation of the name of the document (in Hebrew or Latin), but they are often designated with more popular labels. The *Manual of Discipline* is designated 1QS ("S" stands for the Hebrew term *serek,* "rule"). The *War Scroll* ("The War of the Sons of Light against the Sons of Darkness") is designated 1QM (Hebrew: *milḥama,* "war"); the *Thanksgiving* Scroll, 1QH (Hebrew: *hodayyot,* "hymns of praise"). In addition, 1QSa stands for the *Rule Appendix,* and 1QSb for the *Blessings Appendix,* both regarded as additions to the *Manual of Discipline.* 1QpHab is the *Habakkuk Commentary* ("p" stands for the Hebrew *pesher,* "interpretation"). 4QFl or (Latin: *florilegium,* means "bouquet of flowers") is a thematic collection of biblical passages with commentary, very similar to 4QTest, *Testimonia.* We have also included the *Damascus Document* (CD) among the Qumran scrolls; this name was derived from a statement in the document about "the community of the new covenant in Damascus." Fragments of this document have been found in Qumran, but it was previously known from manuscripts discovered in 1896 in a medieval Jewish synagogue in Cairo. It was probably distributed among Essene camps outside Qumran.

Sirach (= Ben Sira = Ecclesiasticus, abbreviated Sir.), an example of Jewish wisdom literature, written in Hebrew ca. 180 B.C. by Joshua (Jesus) ben Sira, and translated ca. 130 B.C. into Greek by his grandson. It is part of the Old Testament Apocrypha.

Targum ("translation"), is used as a technical designation for Aramaic translations of Old Testament texts. In addition to the large collection of Targums from Babylon (fourth century A.D.) and Palestine (the Jerusalem Targum dates from the sixth century A.D.), there are also older Targums, i.e., the Targum to Job from pre-Christian times (Qumran). They originated because the reading of the Hebrew Scriptures in the synagogue had to be translated for the many who did not understand Hebrew. One of their characteristics is that they are not only translations but paraphrases and interpretations.

Wisdom of Solomon (abbreviated Wis.), is a Greek composition by a Jewish author probably from the first century B.C. The book belongs to the Old Testament Apocrypha (writings included in the Greek Bible, the Septuagint, but excluded from the Hebrew canon of Scripture).

Index